*Laurens De Keyzer*
*Michiel Hendryckx*, pho

# THE OPEN-AIR MUSEUM BOKRIJK

Ludion

Relax and unwind. Isn't it a frequent expression nowadays? If you take time off at Bokrijk Open-Air Museum, that's exactly what will happen. You may agree that we need to rediscover today what it means to relax and unwind. Not so long ago we didn't have a word to describe the condition. Life was lived according to the biorhythms of nature and humankind. Nothing was done in a rush, you didn't have to perform half a dozen things at once, life was unstressed at that time.

Not so today – and it's becoming imperative that we learn how to relax. That's where places like Bokrijk can be a huge help. In Flanders there are few places like this where we can visualise our idea of taking life easier, where the concept gains real meaning and content.

No more talk about relaxation. Experience it for yourself here in Bokrijk. And I do hope that this new guidebook, with its subtle references to contemporary life, will inspire visitors to slow down, look around, consider the past and maybe dare to learn from it. It doesn't matter whether people come to Bokrijk in search of rural beauty, or fascinated by medieval architecture – the museum offers every visitor a total experience. This guide will help you on your way, it gives a clear explanation of routes, tells you about the buildings you see and will provide some exciting new insights.

I should like to thank the museum's curator and all the staff for the indefatigable enthusiasm with which they have worked to produce this guide, together with authors and publisher. I wish the Bokrijk Museum a splendid 21st century and its visitors complete relaxation within the harmony of its setting.

Sylvain Sleypen
*Member of the Executive Council,*
*Province of Limburg, Belgium*

*My house was neither large nor grand*
*Yet was my shelter in this land.*

People are still around in Bokrijk.
You will meet them in the houses,
the barns, the village school, the
churches and windmills. You only
need a little imagination to see
the horse and carts drive past, the
spreading of manure; to hear the
prayers, the sounds of animals and
even the silence before a cock crows.
In every house and barn, even in the
woods, the people of the past are
telling their story to today's visitors.
It is a story of survival. It tells us
how every moment of the day people were at work, praying for work
and working for survival.

All our senses are in use at Bokrijk. They help us to reconstruct life
as it was. It no longer smells of the
unwashed farmer and his wife, or
the pungent odour of ox blood used
to paint the houses and archways.
Instead, the presbytery smells of
cigars, the church of incense, the
farmyard of manure and the fireplaces of peat. The wooden porridge
bowls are still around, and from
Pieter Breugel's paintings we know
that porridge and *stamppot* (mashed
potato and vegetables) were eaten
with a spoon and fingers. There is no
porridge left, its taste is forgotten,
but not the taste of freshly baked
bread, black pudding, bacon and
eggs. Nor the smell of donkeys and
sheep, or the occasional fragrance of
a tree being split in two in the sawpit. Even sounds have been preserved – chiming clocks, windmill
sails turning, horse hooves on cob-
blestones. And for the rest, we can
empathise – simply by looking and
using our imagination.

Bokrijk is a backdrop for day-to-
day living, rather than a museum of
inanimate architecture. Inquiring
visitors who use their knowledge,
senses and imagination, will see
Bokrijk as a time machine of life,
work, and death. Not only does
Bokrijk reverberate with old sayings
and proverbs, with stories from old
folk or simply with nostalgia for the
'good old days', Bokrijk's past also
lives on in the way men and women
today think and act. Visitors who
do not notice must have forgotten
their own forebears, their own
genes.

In Flanders they have this ever-
lasting cliché which calls just about
anything that is pathetic or old-
fashioned *conditions à la Bokrijk.*
But visitors will discover that Bokrijk itself isn't in the least à la Bokrijk.
Born out of a glamorising quest for
the true nature of Flemish identity,
Bokrijk has evolved into the only
'village' in Flanders where time and
space, compressed into 600 years of
life and work, have become a mirror
of ourselves. Sometimes pleasant
to gaze into, sometimes sad. Just as
pleasant and just as sad as looking
at yourself in a mirror. Bokrijk is a
luxurious dip into a life, only a nod
away from our own, a life to which
we are indebted in countless ways.

This guide can only give you
snippets of information and an
incomplete picture of the open-air
museum of the Bokrijk estate.
A visit and your own exploration
will always provide the best picture.

Wickerwork production in the farmhouse from Herenthout

Bokrijk is popularly linked to the 18th-century *Bokkenrijders,* a Limburg gang of notorious highwaymen. However, the name of the estate is completely unrelated. In the Middle Ages it was known as *Buscurake,* meaning a strip of land *(raek, rack)* planted with beech trees *(bouck, bock).*

In 1252 Count Arnold IV sold the estate to the powerful and influential Cistercian nuns of Herckenrode Abbey (at Kuringen, near Hasselt), who in turn leased and cultivated the land until 1797. As a result of the French Revolution the abbey lost its possessions and the church ceased to have any influence over Bokrijk. In the second half of the 19th century an aristocratic family who owned the land had a castle built there, laying out parkland with paths and avenues and planting exotic trees. The estate has remained unchanged to this day, apart from the open-air museum (since 1953) and everything associated with managing a modern recreational centre, including car parks, attractive restaurants to suit all pockets *(Dennenhof, Kasteel* and *Koetshuis),* offices for the administrators and wardens of the estates and recently a new entrance building near the castle. Since 1938 Bokrijk has been owned by the Belgian Province of Limburg.

Bokrijk isn't the first or only museum of its kind. In 1890 similar museums were established in Sweden (near Stockholm) and Norway (near Oslo and Lillehammer), and later in the Netherlands (Arnhem), Denmark (Odense) and Germany (Cloppenburg). They had a similar purpose: to preserve and tell the story of our ancestors by means of architecture and everyday objects. But each site chose a different style of interpretation. Bokrijk has been reconstructed in a similar way to Odense and Cloppenburg. Instead of scattering farmhouses and other buildings around the parkland without any apparent relationship, it was decided to reconstruct an integral community. Thus visitors aren't confronted with unrelated aspects, but with the living and work environment of an entire community, including their old breeds of domestic animals.

In this sense the village of the Kempen (a poor moorland area) is exemplary, even though the addition of the more prosperous farmhouses means it is no longer completely representative. The village has been reconstructed around a triangular village green. In days gone by the sheep of the village were brought in for safety at nighttime. The village offers many other aspects of life in the community – from the pigsty to the smithy, from the bakehouse to the pillory, from the farmhouse to the oil-press. It is a fictitious village, although all the buildings are certainly 'real'. For every building in

Bokrijk one was dismantled from elsewhere.

This visionary and impressive task was largely the undertaking of Jozef Weyns (1913–1974), the first curator of the open-air museum at Bokrijk and already a legend in his lifetime. Tipped off by informants, Weyns travelled around Flanders exploring and investigating interesting but derelict buildings. They would then be dismantled professionally and reassembled in Bokrijk. Consequently around 100 buildings from rural Flanders were rescued in less than 20 years from certain destruction, often with donations and support from local associations. The artist Charles Wellens (1888–1958) also contributed with countless sketches and paintings of many of the Kempen farms.

The curator Mark Laenen also made several interesting reconstructions, including the creation of an educationally and economically viable museum through workshops, courses and exhibitions. He also devoted great attention to the earlier environment of the dwellings. If possible the grounds at Bokrijk would be planted with plants that probably grew in the region at the time.

Nowadays, the emphasis in Bokrijk is on the actual lives of the people that lived in such a community. Dwellings provide information about who lived in them and how they lived. The focus is on the creativity and initiatives of our ancestors as well as the social and economic context. Today, we tend

Boundery stone from Zepperen

Jozef Weyns divided his lifetime's work into three sections, each corresponding to the Flemish landscape. In the poor moorlands he collected buildings from the Kempen of Antwerp and Limburg. In the fertile uplands we wander through Maasland, Limburg Haspengouw and Brabant, and in the fertile lowlands through East and West Flanders.

This guide shows the same subcategories with colours and numbers as you will find in Bokrijk itself. Yellow stands for the Kempen of Antwerp and Limburg , Limburg Haspengouw, the Maasland and Brabant are green; while East and West Flanders are shown in red. The buildings in each farm compound (such as dwellings, barn or bakehouse) which originate from different farms are numbered consecutively, i.e. 2.1, 2.2 etc.

If you begin your tour at the main entrance, the colour is green and at the castle entrance it is yellow. The guide itself moves from yellow, to green and red. The photographs in the guide are easy to identify, but if in doubt each building or feature on site has a colour and number. They can then be easily checked against the ones in the book to gain your bearings.

It is useful to know that the guide doesn't follow a strict route, and visitors are free to choose their own way round the estate. For instance, you may wish to visit the grain-mill first in the Kempen (yellow, no.3) and then turn left to admire a long-gable farmhouse from Houthalen (yellow, no. 23.1). If you prefer to go by colour in consecutive order, i.e. 1, 2, 3 etc., make sure you have the plan with you. We obviously suggest such a route in the guide because we do not want it to look like a maze.

to question history and tradition for their relevance to our present-day lives. We want the past to help us explain buildings and objects, fashions and phenomena of today, in other words to gain a sense of identity from the stories of yesteryear.

The plan of the open-air museum shows a small far corner in brown. This is the 'Old Town' and comprises 17 city dwellings dating from the late 14th to the 16th century which arrived in extremely dilapidated state. Between 1972 and 1989, this part saw a lot of building, but after an investment of some 450 million Belgian francs (1,125,000 euros) the project was halted. The result is a façade of 'old' gables hiding modern buildings and various exhibition spaces so that urban life of the past isn't visually represented in any way. The 'town' is like a mirage in no-man's-land. We will not discuss architectural and other aspects here. The project is unfinished to such great extent that it need not be discussed any further in this guide. Nevertheless we recommend visitors take a look, since it is a remarkable illusory experience. As if chemical warfare has taken place and all that remains standing is the walls. A perfect filmset!

Gateway building from Heers

Cave-hut from Koersel

The writer Victor Hugo, travelling through the Kempen in 1837, wrote: *'The landscape changes between Lier and Turnhout. It looks different, it is no longer rich, verdant Flanders – it is a sandbank, an awkward cinder track, with poor grass, pine plantations, small woods and oak copses, moorlands, the occasional pool, a wild, stark landscape...'*

The peasants on the Kempen had a hard life. Surviving on sandy ground overgrown with heather is far more difficult than on rich polder land. Thus for centuries the homes in the Kempen – the sandy region in the northeast of Flanders – were extremely plain and basic and geared towards utilising any bit of space, any craft and materials. Using only clay and oak or elm wood the peasants constructed buildings of miraculous stability. They first built a framework of wooden trusses. The walls were made by applying stakes and woven rods and then sealing the open sections with interwoven twigs. This was then plastered with a pap of clay mixed with chopped straw, calf hair, horse urine and sometimes dung. Simple yet extremely effective. Only the wealthy farmers could afford to build stronger dwellings with bricks.

As to wealth, visitors may have noticed how big some of the farmhouses can be, although this often is a matter of optical illusion. It was not only the farmer and his immediate family and half the in-laws who lived in the long-gabled farmhouse or farmstead compound with an integral cowshed, but they had to share the space with their animals. Not at the kitchen table, mind you, but the cattle were right there and could be fed directly from the kitchen. Cows would often stand with their heads in the living room, while producing the invaluable manure from their rear end. Chickens and pigs also wandered in and out of the farmhouse, being virtually part of the family. It was only in 1852 that a law was passed banning pigs, rabbits, geese, ducks, pigeons and other fowl from dwellings.

Undoubtedly our modern, highly sensitive nostrils, would have found the smells in such homes almost unbearable. Yet the peasants of long ago couldn't get enough of the stench of manure. What is more, if they didn't have enough and were forced to buy some elsewhere, they would apparently swallow a small sample to make sure they didn't return home with manure that was too runny.

Good muck was essential, especially in the Kempen where they needed three times as much to fertilise the moorland (200 cartloads for one hectare) than, for instance, clay soil. While today we barely know what to do with our enormous mountains of surplus manure, all animal droppings used to be carefully stored in the pit in the cowshed (next to the kitchen). When the time was right the muck would be spread on the poor ground. Thus the peasants chiefly kept livestock to produce muck. Other by-products from the animals would be exchanged for essentials like grain and oil. No part of a pig was wasted. The bladder was used to seal windows, the meat was salted, the hocks smoked in the fireplace, the skin tanned into a superb leather, the bones boiled to make glue, the penis dried to lubricate cogs and wheels, the lard used for cooking and spreading on bread, and the hair to make brushes. Even a pig's vertebrae weren't thrown away since they could be used by the children to play jacks.

The farmhouse was virtually self-sufficient. Within a 100-metre radius of the farm the peasant had everything he needed – clay, wood, straw, flat stones for the floors or well, and so forth. Everyone also organised their own source of energy. The miller benefited from water or wind, the peasant's wife heated the house with wood or turf, the horse kept the horse mill going, the sun shone during the day of course, but at night home-made torches, oil lamps or an edible tallow candle were lit. A cheap solution, but at least the peasant did not depend on a handful of Arab states who can cut off the energy supply of half Europe.

We enter the museum through an early-18th-century gate with blue stone pillars **1**, once the entrance to the *White House* at Kerkom near Sint Truiden.

First you see a so-called 'unlucky cross' **2**, erected to commemorate Joannis Motman, who fell off his horse close by and died on the spot. Since he could not be given the last sacrament, the cross was placed to appeal to the God-fearing passers-by to beg for mercy on his soul. This was not an uncommon event. The inscription on the cross is still legible: HIER IS DOODT GEBLEVEN DEN EERSAMEN JOANNIS MOTMAN DEN 29 MYE 1750. BIDT GODT VOOR SYN ZIEL (Here died honest Joannis Motman on 29 May 1750. God have mercy on his soul).

The powerful grain windmill **3** from Mol-Millegem probably dates from 1788, at least according to an inscription on the old 'claw-iron'. It must have been a tough job reassembling the windmill from scratch, especially as the entire technical construction was left intact and should still be in working order. The mill is supported by four cubes of brickwork with cross-beams. Mills with a brickwork support – or more precisely a stand on which the upper part of the mill pivots – are referred to as 'upright' windmills.

However, no more technical details because they are of such highly specialised jargon, ranging from *runner* and *bedder* to a *shoe* and a *wallower,* that only millers or folklore enthusiasts would make

Kempen village green with view of
the farmhouse-cowshed from Vorselaar

Post mill from Mol-Millegem

much sense of the language. It might even take away some of the visitor's enjoyment. Specialist jargon has been avoided elsewhere in this guide. Visitors with a desire for greater technical specificity should refer to the concise bibliography at the end of this booklet. Others no doubt would prefer a tour of the mill after all, it will be easier to understand this type of mill by looking at it than by consulting a technical drawing.

The most fascinating aspect of this 35-ton upright windmill is that it can turn 360 degrees on its axis, so that it can literally be shifted into the wind. This mill from the Kempen of Antwerp can still be turned around today. But this wouldn't reward the effort since the mill is set amid trees and the sails wouldn't be able to move freely. One interesting commercial detail is that in its heyday the mill could grind 700 kilograms of grain an hour. To put in context: steam-driven mills can process 2,000 kg an hour, working day and night.

The route from the windmill will take you straight to the Kempen village. As was pointed out in the Introduction it isn't a reconstruction of any particular settlement. It is an adaptation of the basic layout of several typical Kempen villages. They all had the characteristic triangular green in their centres - we aren't sure why it should be a triangle – with dwellings and farmsteads grouped around. On the village green (called *dries*) the local herdsman would gather the livestock together for the night. There was always a pond for watering the animals and for dousing any fires in the village.

Many old Dutch sayings now have figurative meanings, e.g. 'straight through the front door into the house' means don't beat about the bush, yet in the farmhouse-cowshed of Vorselaar **4.1**, a reconstruction of a dwelling in which family and cattle all lived under one roof during winter, this is exactly what happened. The Kempen people regarded an entrance or hallway as a waste of space. The living area, also the kitchen, was known as 'the house'. But it is highly unlikely that this house and so many others in Bokrijk looked like this centuries ago. It is all too neat and tidy. There are items hanging on the wall which at the time would have been simply lying around. There is no straw on the floor, the cooking pot no longer reveals its use and there is no washing-up water running out through the drain. The pig's bladder, in which tobacco was stored, or which was

given to children as a ball, hangs awkwardly on the wall. It is as if the former inhabitants are being taught a lesson in 20th-century hygiene.

This is how it has to be in a place visited annually by many thousands of tourists. However it should be mentioned in order to encourage visitors to use their imagination in this interior and see through its sterile atmosphere.

The interior of the Vorselaar kitchen – quite unusual with its built-in oven – partially, but consciously echoes the days of the Flemish painter Pieter Bruegel. In the adjoining interior only objects (and copies) have been preserved or added that are in keeping with 16th-century iconography. One of the more endearing objects here is a large flat basketwork cradle in which the wet nurse and later the mother would feed and care for the baby in front of the fire.

Together with the farmstead they have reconstructed a small barn from Mol-Sluis **4.2** (date unknown). In earlier times the Antwerp Kempen were bristling with such humble buildings. They were useful for storage and had a threshing floor, at right angles to the longitudinal axis of the building, where the farmer threshed the grain with a flail. A cart-shed is built onto the barn, an open but roofed-in space to store small carts.

Farmhouse-cowshed from Vorselaar

pressure on the roof by the formidable east wind. A clever piece of technical insight on the part of our ancestors. Indeed, technically it was quite an art to construct a roof from no more than stalks of corn and rye whose quality weaving and binding could withstand gale-force winds. Those who lived near a river or lake preferred to use reed as it was stronger and more durable, though it did not insulate as well as straw.

Some houses in Bokrijk may easily be described as *roof structures* since they are more roof than walls. But even that was for a reason. The roofs, extending as far as possible over the edges of the walls, prevented the rain from beating against the house and the wind from getting under the roof.

This typifies Bokrijk – from the simplest item to the steepest roof, the museum manifests a celebration of human ingenuity. Today we buy what we need or don't need, or hire a professional to do a job. But not in those days. The people designed and made for themselves what was needed, perhaps with the help of a local artisan. And they wouldn't even consider what was not needed. For even in those days there was enough free time in which to dream – every Sunday and during all the religious festivals. Just as today people grew bored at such times and this led to a huge increase in gambling and games of chance.

Visitors will have noticed that the roof, like so many others in Bokrijk, is thatched and remarkably steep. Flatter roofs were in danger of collapsing, and a steep roof made from straw or reed is ideal for drainage. If, after a few days' rainfall in Bokrijk, you walk up close and touch a thatched roof, you will find that while the water may have soaked the upper layers, it is bone dry underneath. It has been calculated that a thatched roof with a slope of 60 or 70 degrees easily lasts between 60 and 80 years facing south, though only half the time when facing north.

During your walk you may also have noticed that the west side of several roofs slopes more gently than the east side. The so-called streamline theory supporting the design should help avoid too much

The magistrate's bench **5** on the Kempen village green is a silent reminder of justice prior to the French Revolution of 1789. It is actually a copy of the *Groene Vierschaar* from Bevere (Oudenaarde). The accused stood trial, literally, at the bar, a railing or handrail and only the police officers had access behind it. The chair of the court was the sheriff, who represented the landowner in matters of law and order. The sentence was pronounced by the magistrates or councillors. They represented the community, which at that time in Belgian and French assizes had direct joint responsibility for pronouncing punishment. Until the 17th century trials had been a public affair, and according to unwritten law those attending were allowed to discuss and weigh up whether or not the punishment fitted the crime.

When you think of a smithy you tend to think of shoeing horses, but the blacksmith's skills were infinitely more varied. He forged kitchen utensils, nails, irons, weapons, metal dates, wall clamps, garden fences, candlesticks, security bars for trapdoors, cast-iron decoration for fanlights, farming tools – and of course there was all his work and repairs for cartwrights and millers. In fact smithies were the first carriage repairers and as a gesture of recognition to the pioneers of this trade, the Antwerp and Limburg Coachbuilders Federation has supplied the old timber-framed smithy from Neeroeteren **6** with all the appropriate tools. Behind the smithy, built in the mid-19th century and still in use until 1960, you will see the bellows to keep the fire going, and to the right the stable where horses were shod.

Magistrate's bench, a copy of the *Groene Vierschaar* from Bevere (Oudenaarde)

Smithy from Neerouteren

Long-gable farmhouse from Helchteren

Interior of the *Kilbershoeve* from Meeuwen

the deep litter house with pit – where the cattle were kept and the manure was stored – and then the living space with 'house' or kitchen. On the north side there are a large pantry and bedrooms. The flooring is typical of the Kempen of Limburg – large flat stones in the 'house' and small imitation tiles in the living area.

The 'house' or kitchen's ingenious and effective interior is particularly interesting. The heavy cauldron for the cows' fodder, for instance, was too heavy for the farmer's wife to drag or lift. Instead it hung from a swivel post that conveniently swung from the fireplace to the animal troughs built into the kitchen wall. To make butter churning easier, the churn had a rope and a mechanically rebounding hoist fitted to the loft beams. This was a clever mechanism that did the monotonous chore of turning butter in half the time. The farmer's wife pounded the cream with a wooden stick, with a cross or disc with holes attached, until the milk fat coagulated into hard butter. Hot water was frequently added during the process, which took three hours of hard labour, up to three times a week.

Tenant farms like this might appear impressive from the outside, but with barely three hectares of land they were considered small at the time. Apart from the living area and the integral cowshed the farms had few other amenities. Occasionally there would be a pigsty (the one here from Olmen has an adjoining

The exact date of the sheep-pen of *Bettebos* farm at Neerpelt, Limburg **7** is unknown. Though it was usual to carve a date, say, into the wall ties or chisel one into the coping or trusses of the more wealthy farms and houses, no one obviously bothered to do this for sheep or pig pens.

The double-bay, long-gable farmhouse from Helchteren (Limburg) **8.1**, however, is dated. The year 1815 is carved in the chimney breast – a popular place to immortalise snippets of information, proverbs or initials from the owners. The layout of the farm is exactly according to the (Kempen) book, that is, everything under a single roof. The barn is on the west side with a partitioned area for storage and the threshing floor, next comes

*Kilbershoeve* from Meeuwen

latrine **8.2**) and/or oven (this freestanding one without a bakehouse is
from Zonhoven **8.3**). Both buildings
were built later than the farmhouse.

Nowadays we can buy rope at an appropriate shop, but in the past you had one made in the rope yard. Today most of us don't even know what rope is made of, but in former times villagers took some of their own grown hemp to the local ropemaker for him to work with.

The ropemaker's workshop from

mer to tighten the rope and make it firm. In exchange for his fibrous hemp being spun into long, strong rope, the peasant gave the ropemaker money or perhaps some of his own produce.

Today we go to the supermarket for a bottle of oil for the vinaigrette. Our ancestors, however, took their own harvested seeds to an oil-pressing mill. Rapeseed and coleseed were pressed for cooking oil and linseed (or flax seed) for lighting oil or to be mixed into paint.

In the oil-press from Ellikom **10**, an exquisitely maintained example from 1702, still in perfect working order, the seed is crushed between vertical heavy stones that roll over another horizontal one. The bruised seed is then heated in an iron pan over a fire, put into linen bags and beaten while pressed between iron blocks until every last drop of oil is squeezed from the seed.

It was an extremely noisy and dusty production method, even though it began much more unobtrusively on the water side of the mill, where the water set the wheel in motion, the wheel turned the water axle and so on. Until steam was discovered, water was the most important and efficient energy source for mechanised activity. On every river, even on streams that only produced a little water a few months of the year, there was always one windmill at least. The crownwheel of this particular mill bears the inscription: ANNO 1702 DEN 15 MEI HEEFT MESTER P.I. DIT GEMACK (This was made by Master P.I. on 15 May 1702). Only the builder's initials are given – clearly modesty was still an attribute taken for granted in those days.

Ropemaker's workshop from Sint-Pieters-Lille

the Oevelenberg at Sint-Pieters-Lille **9** has been restored extensively and divided afresh into a hackle and spinning area. In the hackle area the ropemaker combed the hemp by drawing it over a small hackle. This was a nasty-looking small plank with several upright teeth over which he would pull the flax or hemp to split the outer husk, remove crooked and short threads and pull the longer ones straight. This could be a menacing instrument when used for less innocent purposes. In the spinning corner the ropemaker and his rope twister spun the rope on an ingenious system comprising a wheel and pinion on a track of 13 wooden combs, which from end to end measured some 140 metres. The ropemaker used a grooved wooden ham-

Oil-press from Ellikom

The *Kilbershoeve* **11** from Meeuwen (Limburg) was one of the biggest and best-known farmhouses of the northern Kempen. It was originally built in the late 17th century as a freestanding two-room dwelling. This is what makes the farm so interesting, since visitors can sense 200 years of life and work from the way the interior and architecture have evolved. Between 1775 and 1780 a stable with a cowshed and threshing floor were added, separated from the kitchen by a passage. The pole with the heavy cauldron arrangement used to feed cattle (the same system as at Helchteren, 8.1) swung from the kitchen through the passage to the feeding troughs. The original front door was moved and the entrance on the southwest corner sealed. In 1900 a one-and-a-half-metre brick extension was added on the west side and bays were built. The farmstead illustrates how the occupants continued to invest in more labour-saving facilities as farming prospered in and around the farm – in 1846 it still had 20 hectares of land. The farmstead also had a bakehouse with a pig pen and a barn with a sheep pen, a threshing floor and storage space for peat and carts.

Most of the house contents were moved along with the farm to Bokrijk. However, Jozef Weyns, the grandmaster of relocating old buildings, wrote in his 1967 guide to the museum that he regretted having to leave certain valuable objects behind. *'Two dozen pewter plates glinted on the rack. But seeing that the Hoydonckx family, the last owners of the farm, were understandably attached to these pieces we were only able to acquire half of them. The rest were made up from our own collection.'*

Visitors are no doubt aware that the farm itself is a great deal older than its contents. For instance the kitchen stove dates from the early 20th century and elicited the following enthusiastic description from Weyns: *'A so-called Leuven stove or kitchen range has been placed in the room. In the 19th century it was an important addition to our rural way of life. The fireplace, from which so much warmth escaped, had its opening closed off, and for the first time in history the farmer could depend on a reliable form of heating in his living quarters. The Kilbershoeve depicts the final chapter in the evolution of the old rural style of life.'*

Weyns is absolutely right. Strolling through Bokrijk we may find the giant fireplaces in many of the farmhouses wonderful to look at and so cosy, but in wintertime they were pretty worthless as a form of heating. Their large size was in order to accommodate all the smoke, which was also used for smoking hams and sausages. But with the smoke went the heat. If you tried to warm yourself from the front, your back was cold, and when you went to bed with only dying embers left, you were liable to see your breath on the wattle-and-daub walls of the room.

At Cloppenburg's open-air museum they conducted an interesting winter experiment. A huge fire was lit in the fireplace of one of the farmhouses, all the shutters were closed and the pens next to the kitchen crammed with animals. The result was that it was barely four degrees warmer than on the outside. Thus the invention of a stove with enclosed heating was a blessing for everyone. The French philosopher and writer Montaigne was in complete agreement – unlike his fellow travellers – when he visited Germany (around 1575). He noted that while the tiled stoves didn't give off much heat, they were at least cleaner than open fireplaces.

Incidentally, the fact that the Kilbershoeve has a chimney is now considered normal, but in Bruegel's time this was more the exception than the rule. In those days fires were mainly stoked up in the centre of the kitchen and the smoke (together with the heat) was drawn up out of the house via a hole in the roof. An example of this can be seen in the oil-press from Ellikom (no. 10).

The attractive 16th century *Hoog-huis* (tall house) from Tessenderlo-Schoot **12.1** looks incredibly sophisticated amid the many other modest dwellings of Bokrijk. It is part of a farm compound and can be seen with a peat store and a large barn, both built later. Constructed in typically Kempen style, it is unusual for the region in that it has an upper storey as additional living quarters. The house was built by a high-ranking army officer who, like a gentleman farmer, enjoyed a certain social standing and could behave like a true lord of the manor.

This is reflected not only by the upper storey, but in the expensive brickwork masonry, including decorative brickwork markings on the outer walls (to protect against calamity?), and a dovecote in the loft. In earlier days the right to keep pigeons, like hunting and fishing, was the prerogative of the aristocracy and the abbeys. However in the 16th century such rights were granted to wealthy tenant farms that had a fixed minimum amount of land. So the owner of this particular house was obviously well off. The pigeons were used as quick and precise mail messengers, but they also were a tasty delicacy and their droppings were highly suitable for growing crops like flax, hops, clover, pot herbs or tobacco. They were a major headache for the local peasants, however, who were forbidden to catch or destroy them. Fortunately the pigeons had to be kept indoors during sowing and harvest periods.

*Hooghuis* from Tessenderlo-Schoot

Peat was stored in the wood and straw building originally from Kalmthout-Nieuwmoer **12.2**. The peat, found in bogs, was cut into lumps, then dried and used for fuel. Peat was the most common source of heating and peasants were allowed to dig out the peat sods from common land, or use a dredger to reach the soggy underlayer. After the turfs of peat had dried they were beaten with a piece of iron into lumps. The peat store from Kalmthout probably dates from the late 18th or early 19th century.

Peat-store from Kalmthout-Nieuwmoer; in the background the *Hooghuis* from Tessenderlo-Schoot

Longitudinal barn from Olen

Tongerlo Abbey once owned no fewer than 126 tenant farms and this fine example at Bokrijk, with original barn and horse-driven mill, is from Oevel (the Antwerp Kempen) **13.1**. The *Uitschool* farmstead in its present form dates from 1735, but its history can be traced back to the early 13th century. The name stems originally from *Udo* and *hole* and literally means *the low lying piece of land of Udo.*

Interestingly, every tenant farmer who lived there between 1393 and 1954, when the farm was finally vacated, can be traced. On the whole they were prosperous farmers. In the 17th century for instance the farm had 45 hectares, about five times as much land as the average tenant farmer was given. The farm's prosperity – 28 oak trees were felled for its beams – is reflected in the brick walls and furnishings. The furniture isn't original but was chosen on the basis of an inventory of the farm drawn up in 1756. Among the handsome pieces was an elm wardrobe, oak kitchen cupboard, clock-case, rural Renaissance cupboard, commode, fashionable display cabinet and dresser with small drawers (plus a secret bottom drawer). Visitors may already have noticed that the main room, like the one in other farmhouse-cum-cowsheds, only had one entrance to the living and kitchen quarters so that it was completely draught-proof in winter months.

The barn from Olen **12.3** dates from 1789, which is inscribed on the support beam in the sheep pen. Folklore specialists refer to this type of building as a 'long' barn when the threshing floor runs along its entire length. The harvesters drove the fully laden cart of hay through the high barn door with the cutaway roof corner. The load was emptied in one of the stacking rooms, then the workers left the barn by a lower door on the other side. So no space or time was wasted. The barn has a purlin roof, the roof covering and rafters directly supported by the purlins or crossbeams that link the trusses. One interesting detail is the fire hook hanging beneath the overhanging roof from 1827. A cross

between a hook and a spear, it was used to push or tear down burning walls. This was a compulsory fire precaution in every village.

Rural women weren't spared even the heaviest or dirtiest work and their position, despite their

Pigsty from Heist-op-den-Berg and
the farmhouse-cowshed from Oevel

major role in the household, wasn't an enviable one. Surprisingly, therefore, at this farm the girls had the privilege of sleeping on the south side of the house, while the boys slept in the cellar. Moreover, the farmer's wife was saved the chore of churning butter – she had an assistant dog. In the deep-litter house next to the kitchen the dog rotated a wheel which, via a crank-shaft that went through the wall into the kitchen, triggered a connecting rod linked to the vertical plunger of the butter churn. Today animal welfare groups would be up in arms about the dog's lot, but for the farmer's wife of yesteryear it was a gift made in heaven.

While we are still in the deep-litter house, you may be surprised to learn just how much manure accumulated from day to day. In February of one year 150 carts were needed to clear the cowshed out, in September of the same year, 120.

Standing alongside the original barn from the same farm – a longitudinal type with threshing floor (similar to 12.3) – there is a 'manege' or horse-driven mill used to operate the threshing machine. The farmstead also has a bakehouse from Oostmalle-Blommerschot **13.2**, probably from the 19th century, and a mid-19th-century double pigsty from Heist-op-den-Berg **13.3**.

During your walk round Bokrijk you will undoubtedly frequently notice that our forebears defecated in pigsties like this one. Relieving oneself was something never done under the same roof as the house,

but in a separate *secreet* (from the French *chambre secrète*) or privy, preferably out of the wind. As well as in or next to a pigsty, this was also done in an annexe next to the bake-house, but never – by government decree – close to a road along which religious processions passed.

Those visitors curious to know how the tenant farmer paid his rent to the abbey will be interested in the following, taken from the farm's yearly records. In 1502 Joannes Verachtert, the tenant farmer, owned half of 5 cows, 6 calves, 4 horses and 40 sheep. In other words, on the sale of any animals half the proceeds went to the abbey, while each party paid half their share for new livestock. The tenant farmer paid a sum of money for the actual farm and ground plus an amount of corn, barley and buckwheat flour.

Servants were chiefly paid in the form of board and lodging, usually sleeping in the barn, although later this arrangement was replaced by money. Around 1900, for instance, when the Uitschool farm still farmed 23.5 hectares (two-thirds of which it owned), the maid earned 9 to 11 Belgian francs an hour, the senior servant 12 to 14 francs and the junior one 8 or 9 francs. Everything seemed to be much cheaper then than now, but this wasn't the case. When the value of bread, a piece of meat or an amount of land is expressed in grams of silver and gold, then the price differences automatically disappear. In fact the real value of manual labour has remained stable throughout the centuries.

Large families are a phenomenon of the last hundred or hundred-and-fifty years. Before then couples, during their reproductive years, had a child only every two or three years. This gap between one child and the next had little to do with contraception. Protracted breast-feeding often kept a woman's menstruation at bay and created temporary infertility. If we also take into account the high infant mortality rate, then we are left with an average of two children per family.

I can also hear the astute reader asking how a farmer from 1900 could care for livestock, take care of the farm and work 23 hectares of land with only a maid and two servants. Of course he couldn't. But then he had thirteen children – that's how he managed.

There is always an exception to the rule and the long-gable farmstead from Heist-op-den-Berg **14.1** is a case in point. Its living room (the winter quarters) is on the west instead of the east side and, contrary to the perceived winter wisdom at the time, has an outer door – perhaps to give certain family members a degree of privacy. The farmhouse also has a kitchen, cowshed and barn all under one roof and is one of the oldest, preserved wattle- and-daub houses from the Kempen. In the lintel above the front door a globe and a cross is inscribed with the year 1679.

In this and other dwellings at Bokrijk you'll notice that the window openings are not sealed with glass, but partly or entirely covered with stretched pig's bladder. Nowadays when this needs replacing, cow bladder is used, since pigs are now slaughtered at a much younger age and their bladders are too small.

The farmhouse has a 17th-century interior, although this is quite similar to a 16th-century one. The panelled cupboard and store cupboard are still there and the table placed in its customary position under the window for light. The barrel churn is fitted with a rebounding plunger for easier butter-making, while the pretty Kempen chairs with straw seats are extra low to make it easier to attend to the fire. It all creates a charming and convivial picture, yet items like these which we now consider lovely to look at were made from purely utilitarian motives at the time. The idea of art

for art's sake didn't exist. We now for instance have sinks of stone or metal to suit any taste or interior-design concept, but in earlier days a sink simply meant a *moo's* – a practical corner with a floor harder than the rest of the kitchen (to take water into account), a bench, rack for dishes and a drain in the wall for dirty water.

Jan Coeckelberghs, the last person to live in the farmhouse until his death in 1952, not only worked on the land but wrote pious, popular verse. His poem *Het Vaderhuis* (The Lord's House) hangs on the wall, while honey presses in the barn recall his beekeeping work.

In the vicinity of the farmhouse is a century-old pigsty from Booischot **14.2**, a slightly older, extremely rudimentary *secreet* or privy from Westmeerbeek **14.3** and a large bakehouse from Heist-Goor **14.4**. A small pigsty and bedroom were added to the bakehouse wall for guarding the pigs in wartime. Countless loaves of bread were obviously baked here, but four children were also born on the premises. In 1910 their father died in the insalubrious small bedroom next to the pigsty.

Interior of the long-gable farmstead from Heist-op-den-Berg

Barn of the long-gable farmstead from Heist-op-den-Berg

Rear side of the long-gable farmstead from Heist-op-den-Berg

During its time the bakehouse we just visited served as an inn and was used for parties, but in no way can it compete with the stunning country inn *In Sint-Gummarus* from Lier **15.1**. For the convenience of visitors to Bokrijk, the inn's dividing walls were removed to make a large spacious bar where drinks and regional food are served. The rest of the inn has been restored to its original 1900 appearance. The inn originally comprised a bar room and living quarters on the south side and a cowshed and barn built at right angles on the west wide. Facing north were two cellars and the baking oven. In the present bar room the fireplace comes from the *Kruiningen* farm at Deurne (Antwerp).

In the inn's yard visitors can try their hand at archery or enjoy a traditional game of skittles – in the skittle-alley it is still played with the customary ninepins, a memory of a bygone age. There was so much gambling on skittles – especially among America's immigrants – that it was forbidden in the United States. However, inventive minds then devised a game with ten skittles, arranged in a triangular rather than a diamond shape. In its legal form the American army reintroduced skittles to Europe and the 'new' game gradually superseded the old.

Country inn *In Sint-Gummarus* from Lier

There is also a pall-mall game at the inn in which the player tries to drive heavy balls with a mallet through an iron ring.

In the museum grounds generally enthusiasts are able to play many traditional or now virtually extinct games, from shuffleboard to climbing the greasy pole, from tug-of-war to walking on stilts. These popular games offer a wealth of Flemish sayings and proverbs to interest both linguists and amateur lovers of language. But that applies to Bokrijk in general: the museum provides so much information on how our language of today is deeply rooted in the history of our forebears.

The presbytery from Schriek **16** lies behind a high garden wall flanked by stables and carriage sheds. This delightful pastor's dwelling was built in 1776 and was transported to Bokrijk in a dilapidated state in 1968. Six years and 150,000 euros later it has been restored to all its former glory. Glory is the appropriate word here. On his appointment, the successor to Pastor Adrianus Snoeckx, who had the house built, acknowledged that 'God's servant was better housed than God himself'. He then set about raising funds to build a new and larger church. And in this he was successful. The imposing church now stands in Schriek, while at Bokrijk a small church from Erpekom has been rebuilt close to the old presbytery.

In some Flemish villages to this day an elegant presbytery still stands detached and aloof from the other neighbouring houses. The difference now is its solid bourgeois style when compared to the architectural banality of so many dwellings, whereas in the rural past such houses were built by the church as an expression of power and authority. Then the building materials and architectural style of these 18th- and 19th-century presbyteries with their richly furnished interiors and box-tree and walled gardens stood out magnificently against a backdrop of humble farm dwellings. Sometimes a moat would be built around a presbytery and this only served to widen the distance between the religious authority and their poor illiterate sinful flock.

The layout of the presbytery is typical of others found in the Kempen and is based on an 18th-century town house. To the right of the entrance is a large living room, with a reception room, kitchen, cellar and cellar-room on the left. The 'best' room is decorated with motifs which recall the Rococo style.

Presbytery from Schriek

The kitchen of the presbytery from Schriek

Barn from Olen

Farmhouse *Zelse Schrans* from Herenthout

Unfortunately the original murals – a crucified Christ above the chimneypiece and portraits in a landscape on the walls – as well as all the paintings on the ceilings of the ground floor have disappeared. Two pike (*snoek* in Dutch) can be seen swimming on the fine staircase, a knowing reference to Snoeckx, the builder.

One of the most striking items of furniture is the elegant 17th-century Baroque cabinet in inlaid black ebony. While the interiors of the farms were purely utilitarian right down to the smallest objects, the more wealthy and sophisticated clergy and burghers were already preoccupied with refined buildings and matching furniture design. Moreover there was no lack of convenience – even in his kitchen Pastor Snoeckx was better off than his parishioners. Here there is not only a large cast-iron kitchen range with an oven and built-in cooking pot, but one of the earliest examples of a refrigerator.

While the pastor's flock was spoon-fed, he used a fork. Unlike today soup and main course were eaten from the same plate and this was simply turned upside down for the dessert. It is unknown whether the pastor drank wine or beer with his meal, though peasants never drank with their food. Instead they drank beer before the meal to gain an appetite and after the meal to aid digestion. Water, because of its dubious quality, was not used for drinking purposes.

Little is known about the *Zelse Schrans* farmhouse from Herent-

Farmstead from Wortel, now the Museum Shop

hout **17**. In the brickwork on one of the side walls you will see the date 1652, but perhaps the building is older and at one time was half-timbered. However the stripes of whitewash on the front brickwork are unrelated to this conjecture. They simply imitate the white stone layers often found in town houses. In the house itself visitors will be charmed by the fireplace – another example from the *Kruinigen* farm at Deurne (15.1).

The elegant decorative door frame of the farmstead from Wortel **18** won't have escaped visitors' notice. The house with its L-shaped layout dates from around 1730 and was once used as an inn. It has now been converted to Bokrijk's museum shop, while the large three-bay

In the old villages of the Kempen the church was not located on the village green, so in Bokrijk the small Romanesque church from Erpekom **20** was built at a distance from the green, which was reserved as a meadow and gathering point for livestock. The church from Erpekom, a hamlet of Grote-Brogel, is a gem of simplicity. First there was the simple rectangular nave, without pillars, with stone walls barely 2.5 metres high and with a solid wood construction for the roof. That's what the church looked like in the 12th century. A hundred years later a choir was added and the walls of the nave were made higher. The tower was added in the 16th century, where the original entrance to the church was located. The original door is now on the south front.

The first thing you notice about the church is the robust roof construction based on a Romanesque roof truss – each rafter rests on a tie beam – and the absence of a pulpit, confessional boxes and communion rails. The latter is unrelated to neglect or iconoclasm, but correctly refers to church interiors before the Council of Trent (1545–1563).

What you also notice is that the church walls were originally plastered, but are no longer. The committee involved with the church's reconstruction at the time was unable to reach a unanimous verdict on this. Most visitors, however, prefer to see the walls the way they are. The colour and texture of the old masonry help create a sense of absolute authenticity: this is how the church looked at its inception. Moreover the plastered walls were originally decorated with a series of murals and now that these have all but disappeared there seems little point in painting them again. In Erpekom at least one such mural has been saved, possibly relating to Saint Hubert, patron saint of the church. He is commemorated in a

Barn from Wortel; in the background the church from Erpekom

barn next door is used for temporary exhibitions.

A little further along, near the small church, there is a reconstruction of a wooden pillory **19**, where on market day the offender, with his/her neck chained to the pillory, would be denounced and mocked by the local community. A sign would be displayed bearing the offender's name and crime, while at the foot of the pillory was a symbol of the offence for those unable to read. The pillory remained in the Penal Code even after the French Revolution, but hasn't been used in Belgium since the first half of the 19th century. The Netherlands abandoned this form of punishment in 1854. But the idea behind it didn't disappear

with the pillory, as many female collaborators found to their cost after the Second World War. They were shaved bald and dragged or driven around the streets at the mercy of the booing and jeering crowds of onlookers.

sculpture group by Jan van Steffenswert, dated 1510. Before leaving the church please admire the splendid carved head of the Virgin Mary, attributed to Master van Elsloo in the early 16th century. For lovers of boxes, chests, cases, or anything else that opens and closes, under the tower is a chest carved from a tree

Interior of the church from Erpekom

trunk with heavy iron fittings and three locks. In this, church records and money were stored. Sometimes provisions were stored in the church such as hams and chests of grain. These weren't extras for the church wardens, however, but for villagers in time of war, seeking refuge in the church, the only stone building in the village.

Church from Erpekom with the pillory

Rear side of the cave-hut from Koersel

Seen in terms of our own affluence, we imagine life as it appears at first glance in Bokrijk to be an impoverished one. Yet, under normal circumstances rural people were in clover as far as food supplies were concerned. Even when harvests were bad the abbey always had food stocks secreted away for its unfortunate tenants. A sense of solidarity among people was far greater then than it is now. Not only did villagers help each other during harvest time or when building and repairing homes and barns, but they all sat down at the same table when a pig was slaughtered. No doubt this had less to do with altruism than the golden rule about giving and receiving. Whatever the case, it reveals that farmers and their families often had it much better than we naively assume that a straw roof and mud floor indicate.

At the same time the proverbial grinding poverty certainly existed and was often passed from one generation to the next. At Bokrijk you can almost physically experience this in the so-called cave-hut from the Limburg Koersel **21**. This is a reconstruction of a dwelling partly built underground, based on sketches by Charles Wellens, and at the time was still inhabited by a hermit.

This extremely small and low hovel consists of the semi-underground living area and an attached bedroom. The poorest people of the moorlands, like the broom-makers, had to make do with a hole in the ground with loose stones for the floor, straw for the roof and wattle and daub for the low walls. The wattle-and-daub chimney here is smeared with (fireproof) clay. Apart from certain workers' dwellings in the cities, this is the most primitive form of housing to have survived in the Kempen. In the 19th century semi-underground hovels like this were still quite common.

In the living area of this one is a so-called *papblok* – part of a tree

Field chapel from Lummen

trunk with hollows gouged out. Whether buckwheat *pap,* that is porridge, was eaten with the hands from these, or the hollows were used to hold plates seems hardly relevant amid such squalor.

A little further along, in the direction of the large grain mill, you come to a field chapel from Lummen **22**, which in 1963 had to make way for the building of a motorway. It is said that wherever you go on Flemish roads you encounter the Virgin Mary and it is the same in Bokrijk, from the moorlands to the lowlands. The Virgin Mary was the ultimate hope, although for every ailment people had a different saint worshipped with scapulars, devotional prints, reliquaries and, of courses, sculptures. In Bokrijk you meet stone versions of Saint Arnold, Saint Anthony and Saint Rock.

When you take a right at the chapel you come across one of Bokrijk's first acquisitions – a small farm from the second half of the 18th century, which was transferred from Houthalen-Kwalaak to the estate in 1953 **23.1**. Between 1897 and 1919 one Martinus Rekkers and his niece lived here. They owned two hectares of farmland and three cows. That doesn't seem so labour-intensive by today's standards, but even with the cows producing around 18 litres of milk every three days meant butter had to be made every two or three days.

The layout of the farm is already familiar to visitors. The interior is furnished as it was in 1919, the year Martinus Rekkers died. A labour-saving discovery in the cowshed is the butter mill, so we may assume that the continual butter-making process in the Rekkers household was not so exhausting after all. This churn was driven by one of the dogs chained to the cowshed wall.

On the same site the 200-year-old bakehouse from the pastor's farm at Eksel **23.2** was rebuilt. The building is larger than that found on similar types of farms but in this case it also housed pigs.

Long-gable farmhouse from Houthalen-Kwalaak

Interior of the *Wellenshoeve* from Lummen

The *Teuten* house from Eksel

The pioneers of Bokrijk not only survive through their drawings and writings, but have been immortalised on the museum site itself. A monument to Jozef Weyns stands at the entrance to the museum, while artist Charles Wellens gave his name to the *Wellenshoeve* **24**, the first building to rise up from the site in 1952 – under the most magnificent oak tree. In many aspects the build-

ing was an experimental adaptation of the artist's Arcadian dream.

The basic layout of the farmhouse is similar to the *Engelen* farm from Lummen and is typical of the Limburg Kempen: from east to west, living room, kitchen, cowshed and barn. It also has the traditional large cobbled floor in the kitchen, and a mosaic of small pebbles in the 'best' room.

Incidentally, during my own youth in East Flanders the 'best' room in our urban house was a separate salon, but my mother – not a farmer's daughter from the Meetjeslandse polders for nothing – always referred to it as 'the clean place' or simply 'the place'.

The interior of the farm is furnished from the artist's own 19th-century collection, although the building was originally from the 18th century. He added a butter mill and a bay to the historic structure to enhance the romanticised ideal people had of the Kempen in 1950.

Charles Wellens was present when the museum was formally opened on 12 May 1958. Three months later, aged 70, he died in the town of Hasselt.

More accurate historically and certainly more interesting than the farmstead of Wellenhoeve is the so-called *Teuten House* from Eksel, Limburg, built in 1731 **25**. As the Michelin Guide would put it: *mérite un détour!*

An uncomplimentary word in Dutch for a woman who is a sourpuss, is *teut*. But the erstwhile Teuten were no moaners, though without doubt there were some sharp tongues among them. However, it seems that the origin of the name of this travelling group of tradesmen is unclear, although the name may have been initially used as a profanity in Dutch towns and later adopted by the Teuten. Having organised themselves into companies the Teuten worked, among others, as tinkers and horse doctors as well as cutting and buying hair. The Teuten from the Kempen, Dutch Limburg, North Brabant and the Land of Loon, now called Belgian Brabant, operated chiefly in the Netherlands, northern and central Germany, Alsace-Lorraine, Luxembourg and Denmark. Each company was in charge of its own trading region, operating according to a meticulous system of shared labour. They had their own dialect and distinct style of dress, ethical code, customs, written contracts and unwritten agreements. Some of them, such as the textile merchants, grew to be immensely wealthy, living a bourgeois life in luxurious farmsteads. They would withdraw to these homes at least once a year, in the harvest season and/or during winter.

They were a tough bunch, they had to be, travelling huge distances along difficult and often dangerous roads with enormous loads on their backs. They earned themselves a good name far and wide with their honest dealings and courteous behaviour. In the countryside they would be greeted with open arms when they arrived each year, because their prices were so competitive and there were no strings attached. They had a very reliable credit system for their customers – possibly theirs was the earliest enterprise to create 'brand' loyalty!

So as the years went by the Teuten developed into a major dynasty, with wealthy citizens, landowners and people with private incomes. But developments in the 19th century gradually corroded their way of life. As a result of the growing competition, modern methods of transport, and changing national boundaries their remarkable trading empire ground to a halt. The textile Teutens managed to make it into the 20th century. Some invested their capital in the first factories, leather tanneries, laundries or cigar factories. But for those from the Kempen the end was in sight and they failed to withstand the competition from their great rivals the Tötten in German Westphalia. The textile Teutens from Germany radically reorganised themselves and established large trading centres in the northern Netherlands which became highly successful. Today they are an intrinsic part of our commercial heritage: department chains like Cloppenburg, C&A or Vroom & Dreesman are their direct descendants.

Our visitors will scarcely be surprised to see that the Teuten house brought to Bokrijk in 1966 stands out sharply from the other farmsteads on this side of the village square regarding size, building materials and interior finishing.

Interior of the the *Teuten* house from Eksel

It is an elongated brick building with a curved gable. Here, unlike all the other farmsteads in Bokrijk, you don't enter straight into the main room. A corridor leads to a living room on the left and on the right into a room that has been re-created to look like a village shop. The whole house is redolent of comfort and good taste, from the magnificent kitchen cupboard to the oak cabinet in the living room. Lest all this bourgeois adornment should tempt you to forget that many of the Teuten families were also farmers, on the right of the living quarters and under the same roof are the byre, barn, stable and cart-shed.

In an article that appeared in the magazine *Kunst en Cultuur* (1998, no. 33), the present curator of the Bokrijk Open-Air Museum, Annick Boesmans, writes: *'There are four reasons for defending the existence of a museum like Bokrijk. First, there is the setting: it's a place where everyone can feel at home. Then it shows us how we, society as a whole, have advanced. The other two reasons are that it is beautiful, providing a sense of peace, and finally there is the emotional impact of simplicity.'*

These are four very good reasons to visit Bokrijk, with the understanding that it reveals fascinating aspects of the past and human ingenuity. This covers a wide range, from the delight you may experience in a discovery – take for instance the attractive and well-designed baby-walkers for toddlers which you encounter in several of the farmsteads – to the understanding and interpretation of complicated architectural or other techniques. And those interested in cooking and/or alternative medicine will be fascinated by the herb gardens, where they will find plants that have been carefully cultivated down the centuries.

The herb garden **34** – which has been moved from the spot where now you find a vegetable garden **26** – provides Bokrijk with a selection of herbs that are still used today for various purposes. Also, there are many plants that we no longer use, unless we still believe that the houseleek protects a house from being struck by lightning, or that the perennial herb lady's-smock, also called cuckoo flower, helps prevent infertility. Formerly, cures for sickness were largely based on herbal remedies and the study of plants. In the 17th and 18th centuries botanists and medical students would often undertake lengthy expeditions in search of new types of plants. The well-to-do would bring home exotic shrubs and plants from their foreign expeditions and cultivate them on their estates. Every major city would have its own Botanical Gardens, containing herbs, unusual shrubs and trees. Bokrijk invites you to glimpse the collections of our ancestors, the glamorous plants from foreign lands as well as the indigenous plants that grew here long ago. Enjoy their fragrance, but please don't pick them.

Grain-mill from Lummen-Rekhoven

The date ANNO 1697 is written on one of the tie beams of the barn from Lommel-Kattenbos **27**. The barn looks like someone has pulled their hat over their eyes. It's a straw hat. Like so many of the farmhouses and barns at Bokrijk this thatch is crowned by a roof ridge on which strips of turf have been turned upside-down and secured with wooden pins. In this way the farmers kept the sides of the roof in place. Nowadays this is done with U-shaped ridge tiles; formerly it was achieved by using grasses and heather whose roots grew into the thatch. The turfs, measuring 40 x 60 x 90 centimetres were placed partially overlapping along the roof ridge, and in time grew into one continuous stretch. This also had the great virtue of absorbing water and retaining it for some while. The water absorption helped keep the plants alive on the roof ridge, and it is interesting to note that between the water-retaining grasses people would plant houseleeks, presumably as a none-too-efficient protection against thunder and lightning. The Flemish poet Guido Gezelle (1830–1899) in his poem *Sempervivum tectorum L* (1894) dedicated several inspired verses to these remarkable roofs.

Nearby you can see how, before the arrival of mechanised tools, people sawed tree trunks into manageable planks. One man would stand in a sawpit **28**, another above on the scaffolding, and the two of them would operate a frame saw, each holding one end. Houses required considerable quantities of wood in their construction and the sawpit was an essential in the village. To obtain wood suitable for sawing, the trees would first be allowed to 'die on the trunk', i.e. upright. After that they would either be chopped into square beams, using a woodcutter's axe and adze, or else they would be sawn along lines that had been previously marked on the wood with blacking. The sawpit here in Bokrijk is a reconstruction. Likewise, the grain mill from Lummen-Rekhoven **29** has been reassembled from various sources. The entire milling machinery comes from the *Rooier* mill at Gruitrode after its wheel broke in 1956. There are many excellent descriptions of how these water mills worked. In Bokrijk you can actually see the mill in action, and the ground meal emerging. The mill from Lummen is what is called an 'undershot' type, which means that the water pushes on the paddles at the bottom. The output from this type of wooden water-driven wheel is fairly small since it only makes use of the force of the fall of water on the paddles.

In the light of all that has been said, it would seem that the attitude for visitors to adopt as they end their stroll through the landscape of the old Kempen, is one of pious respectability. We begin beside an iron crucifix from Kaulille **30** which was erected somewhere between Roermond and Diest in the course of the 19th century, at the spot where someone had been murdered. Sometimes called a 'kissing cross', it was also known, without any euphemism, as a 'murder cross' and would be paid for by the person who had committed the crime. When the carriage bearing the coffin arrived at the cross, the coffin would be lifted off the bundles of straw it was resting on and the straw left behind at the cross. The coffin was then transferred onto the pallbearers' shoulders and carried by foot the rest of the distance. A short way on, we pass a plaster cast of a wooden wayside crucifix **31** which was placed sometime during the 19th century in Molenbeersel close to the Belgian-Dutch border. And should you wish to beseech divine clemency for the most unscrupulous miller of them all, make your way to the statue of the Virgin Mary in one of her chapels from Westmeerbeek **32**, a small neoclassical brick building dating from 1845, with an altar in Louis-XVI style.

Then, after godliness comes some relaxation.

Right at the other side of the Kempen, not far from the little hut, the visitor can admire an archer's mast from Booischot **33**. If the family was the cornerstone of society, then one of the cornerstones of the local community was the archery club. The earliest reliable sources we have about these clubs date from the 13th century. They probably originally operated as a form of local militia. It is known that they sometimes functioned as a village guard against outside attack. The clubs had their own festivals and distinctive customs at weddings and funerals. When members of the club fell sick, they would provide support and collected charity to care for widows and orphans. Like the medieval guilds they had their own statutes and laws. They lasted until the French Revolution, when they were banned because they were so intricately associated with the *ancien régime.* Not surprisingly, the French weren't too keen on having groups of trained and practised gunmen in the territories they were occupying. For some of the militia bands, that was the end of the story. But others were re-founded after 1814. Today there are still many of these groups, some still shooting with longbow or crossbow and holding archery competitions. But judging from the names of the clubs, occupying armies need no longer fear them. Indeed, the archery mast from Booischot was presented to Bokrijk by the archery society called *Ons genoegen* (Our Pleasure).

A point of interest: on the first floor of the presbytery from Schriek (no. 16) there is a splendid collection of silver trophies and decorative chains associated with the world of archery clubs.

## BRIEF HISTORY

Down the centuries millers have had a bad press. Possibly this was because they had to earn their living by taking a cut from every sack of flour they ground. The size of the scoop they used would be decided with each individual customer. But evidently many farmers felt cheated, and in medieval literature there are countless stories and rhymes in which the miller is presented as a thief and a cheat. One saying in Dutch goes 'There's never a miller's rooster that doesn't eat stolen grain' and there are countless variations on this theme. It seems that although weavers and tailors were known to cheat with the measures of cloth they sold and the amount of thread they charged for, millers took the prize for petty larceny. As late as 1896 we find the story of Alfons De Cock (in the journal *Volkskunde, Tijdschrift voor Nederlandsche Folklore,* Ghent, vol. 9, p. 146): *'Even today millers bear the brunt of popular teasing and tormenting and are accused of taking too full a scoop out of the flour they have ground.'* In Dutch today there are many sayings and double-entendres contributing to the bad name of millers, all attesting to this image of the lewd and corrupt figure. A severe saying in Dutch is *'Someone who holds the sack is as bad as the person who fills it',* implying that an accomplice is as bad as the thieves themselves.

Farmhouse-inn from Ulbeek

# THE LIMBURG HASPENGOUW AND THE MAASLAND THE 'FERTILE UPLANDS'

The way you view the village of Bokrijk is completely up to you. The guidebook simply suggests a route, using colours and numbers. Curiously, you may find that if you walk around with the guidebook in hand, following the numbering of the buildings as much as possible, you sometimes feel a little lost or confused. The walk through the Kempen starts at the castle entrance but should you wish to visit the Haspengouw region the numbering suggests you return to the museum's main entrance. This is not necessary. However, having visited the Kempen, should you prefer not to walk backwards, from number 25 to number 1 in the Haspengouw, but instead from number 1 to 25, I recommend the following. Return to the church of Erpekom, turn down the long straight road leading away from the Kempen towards the main entrance. Then you'll come upon number 1, coloured green, and you can begin at the beginning.

The layout of the Kempen village at Bokrijk is inspired by historical examples taken from former Kempen settlements. However, when constructing the section to reflect the Haspengouw region it was decided to make a faithful copy of an existing village. The choice fell on the village of Ulbeek, today part of Wellen, as it is shown by the mid-19th-century land registry. It should be pointed out that with one exception, the actual houses don't come from Ulbeek. What was copied was the environmental planning as it then was. The Haspengouw region lies in central Belgium, south of the Kempen, stretching towards the valleys of the Meuse and Sambre. It is one of Belgium's most fertile districts. Today there are still large farmsteads half-hidden like pearls between the rolling fields and meadows. The southern part of the Haspengouw region of the province of Limburg is composed of dry, gentle hills. The landscape is wide and open, the layers of clay and loessial soil are rich and fertile. Here the farmsteads are large and the villages small, concentrated clusters of buildings. The northern part of the region, termed the 'Humid Haspengouw', presents a landscape of rivers, springs, spongy meadows and woodland, ideal for cattle and fruit farming.

The farmsteads in southern Haspengouw usually belonged to a castle, an abbey or a *commanderie,* the seat of a commander of an order of knighthood. The farmsteads here are different from those in the Kem-

pen. In southern Haspengouw the imposing farm compounds, and later also the smaller farms, were usually in the form of a square: the farmhouse, barn, cowsheds and entrance gate arranged around an inner courtyard. Occasionally there would be an exception to this rule, and the house might stand separately from the other buildings.

Every cloud has a silver lining, and that's certainly true of the gateway building from Heers 1. It's composed of two living areas from an imposing quadrangular Limburg farmstead. The main road between Liège and Brussels was being widened and the farmstead had to be, as it were, 'beheaded'. Incidentally, this fate befell quite a few farms and country seats as Belgium became thickly threaded with concrete and asphalt for the sake of the advancing motor-car. Happily, the Belgian Ministry of Public Works had the wisdom to donate the decapitated farm building to Bokrijk in 1957. This called forth appreciative words from the curator Jozef Weyns: *'We have been given a suitably impressive entrance building for the Haspengouw section of our museum.'* On the left of the gateway is the original farmhouse dwelling, probably dating from the first half of the 18th century. The gateway itself and the dwelling on the right were added in 1774, the date being chiselled into the keystone in the arch of the gate frame.

A short way on you come across another victim of the widening of the Liège-Brussels highway, from

Tollhouse from Gelinden

the village of Gelinden **2**. This attractive building in the typical brick and blue-stone Haspengouw style was inhabited up to the time it was moved to Bokrijk. It would seem, however, that the building wasn't originally intended as a dwelling. It was most likely used as a tollhouse at one time and for this purpose was placed (in 1725?) at the edge of what was then the highway from Liège to Sint-Truiden. The custom of paying toll for road use stems back to Merovingian times (c. AD 430–751). The money was collected by a toll-master and was used initially for road maintenance. This was essential, since deep cartwheel ruts, large muddy pools, and other inconveniences made travelling a hazardous undertaking until well into the 18th century. So difficult were the roads that for heavy carriages a span of ten or twelve horses would be used. In Bokrijk today you walk along a cobbled street, painfully challenging to any visitor in high heels, but a blessing for the transport vehicles of former days – provided they didn't exceed the maximum weight per type of cart as stated in the imperial decree of 1806. Having paid the toll – which also depended on the vehicle's axle width – the wooden barrier would be opened and you drove through. The barrier here in Bokrijk is an exact copy of the first barrier at Gelinden, dating from 1723.

Close to the large museum car park near the main entrance is the renovated wash house from *Ter Beek* Abbey in Metsteren (Sint-Truiden) **3**. This old laundry, built about

30 years ago, was restored in 1967. It was built in 1731 over the Melster-beek stream so that the nuns could do their washing in clear running water under cover. With an eye to historical accuracy, when the building was restored in Bokrijk it was also constructed over a brook – the Kapelle. Today, however, it houses toilet facilities for visitors.

You pass by the small pillar chapel from Klein-Gelmen built in 1771 **4** and a boundary stone used from 1553 to mark the border between the legal districts of Zepperen and Sint-Truiden **5**, before reaching a half-timbered field chapel from Kortessem **6** constructed in 1778. Maybe at this stage one of your children will be protesting vociferously against this unwelcome expedition. No problem – say a little prayer for help by this small chapel, known in Dutch as a 'crying chapel', where in olden days many mothers made a pilgrimage if their children cried too much. The success rate, however, is none too clear. Our ancestors commonly sent up prayers to heaven in times of distress or danger. But it isn't clear what prayer was recited by the ancient stone cross that once stood beside the old Diepenbeek highroad **7**. On the other hand, the cross of Velm **8** bears an inscription from the 1590s that makes all apparent: it is a prayer beseeching heaven to have mercy upon the soul of a pious man who was murdered here (AL DVER EEN MORDADIG WERCK).

Wash house from the *Ter Beek* abbey in Metsteren

One of the earliest acquisitions of Bokrijk Museum was the *Contzen-winning* 9. It was bought in 1957 from the then hamlet of Klein-Hoe-selt, and meticulously dismantled, to be carefully reconstructed at Bokrijk. The Limburg dialect word for a farm is *winning* and in this case the farm belonged to one Bernard

Third Crusade in 1190 as the 'Broth-ers of the hospital of Our Lady of the Germans in Jerusalem.' It offered hospitality to pilgrims from the Holy Roman Empire. Eight years later the brotherhood became an order of knighthood and continued to fulfil its highly commendable charge from the pope and Holy Roman Emperor of welcoming pilgrims and caring for the sick.

As early as 1241 the small farm-house now known as the Contzen-winning, together with the estate o Damereis, became the property of Alden Biesen. With its richly wooded expanses, the land was commercially highly desirable. This was still the case when in the 18th century Bernard Contzen became chief forester, employed to watch over the woodland day and night, plant saplings in felled areas, organ-ise the sale of wood, prevent dam-age to trees, commercial timber and wildlife, confiscate poached game and weapons, and hand over to the commander anyone found breaking the regulations. Punishment for poaching was often severe, but the heaviest sentence – a compulsory pilgrimage on foot to Santiago de Compostela, imposed at the special request of the forester – was reserved for those who stole wood. Such a sentence indicates the importance of wood production at the time. It was used as fuel and heating in kitchens and for building houses, ships, fences, barracks, estate and property boundaries, and for many other purposes.

In 1789, more than five centuries after the estate and farmhouse were acquired by Alden Biesen, the story ended. The Revolutionary French dissolved the German Order, seized the property of the *commanderie* and sold the woodland and stock-piles of wood. Willem Contzen, son and successor to his father, tried with heart and soul to ward off the evil hour, praying 'most fervently

Visitors will undoubtedly have noticed by now that the beds in these houses would be a bit cramped for the average Westerner of today. Quite simply – our ancestors were smaller than us. In 1863 the Bel-gian army announced that the minimum height for soldiers would be reduced from 1.57 to 1.55 metres. That sounds to us like rather short soldiers.

Formerly people used to sleep in a sitting position, supported by cushions and bolsters. It has been suggested by some historians that the reason for this was that lying flat reminded them of death, which they wished to avoid. Far more plausible is the notion that it made belching that much easier: it was customary to have a large and, by our standards, generally heavy meal before going straight to bed. And as anyone who has had children will remember – no comfy sleep without a good burp first. In fact it's difficult for us to imagine how our ancestors used to sleep. Until well into the 18th century communal sleeping was the norm and there was no notion of per-sonal privacy. In public lodging houses and inns it was generally cus-tomary for complete strangers to snuggle in bed together. With this proviso – if your travelling companion was of a higher social class, out of pure politeness you were expected to ask which side of the bed they preferred to sleep on.

In many farmsteads the bed stood firmly in the middle of the room, with neither niche nor secluding curtains. In the small recess-es found in rooms from the 16th century on, generally built against the walls of the animals' stalls, later against the wall by the fireplace, there was just room for two people to lie, squashed up against each other, or if need be on top of one another. Not until the mid-19th century were beds placed in a separate sleeping room – with a door and lock. With this migration of the bed, and partly under pressure from the Christian Church, the place of sex also migrated, changing from a normal activity into a taboo subject.

Contzen. In 1756 he was appointed forester and tax-collector for the woodlands which, at Beverst and Diepenbeek, were owned by the *commanderie* of Alden Biesen, seat of the so-called German Order. This Order was founded during the during the High Mass' that he might be sick on the actual day of sale. To no avail. Interestingly, the Contzen family continued to live in the farmhouse until the mid-20th century.

The house called Contzenwinning, now at Bokrijk, has undergone considerable rebuilding, and is thought to date in its present state partly from the 16th century, partly from 1718 (according to a dated stone in the attic of the main house), and partly from the 19th century. The buildings don't follow the classical south-Limburg style of an enclosed square, but are grouped around a dung-heap.

The farmhouse is particularly interesting due to the contrast between the interior of the tenant's house and that of the owner. On the north side at right angles to the main dwelling a small ground-floor 'apartment' was built with two rooms. This was where the estate's land agent, for instance, could lodge if so desired, or have something to eat and drink when he came to collect the rent. Compare the two interiors: that of the tenant contained simple elm-wood chairs around a plain solid table, while the guest's apartment has elegant chairs of black painted beech with wickerwork seats around a beautiful circular table. Furthermore, the land agent had an Empire-style bed and various items of furnishing of greater refinement than what stood in the tenant's quarters. Nor should we forget to mention the relative privacy in which he could perform his toilet – a suspended latrine on his bedroom wall enabled him to relieve himself directly outside and deposit his worthy offering straight into a barrel standing against the half-timbered outer wall of the house.

Rear side of the *Contzenwinning* from Klein-Hoeselt

Interior of the *Contzenwinning* from Klein-Hoeselt

'Apartement' in the *Contzenwinning* from Klein-Hoeselt

In 1971 the journal *Ons Heem* (no. 25) published a detailed description of the *Duifhuis* **10**, an imposing square farmstead from the hamlet of Bernissem (Sint-Truiden). In conclusion the author writes: *'What with new agricultural methods and the regrettable decline in the farming business it gradually became impossible to maintain this large farmhouse, and over the past few years it grew more and more dilapidated. Indeed, the building would have been written off, had it not been for the timely intervention of an open-air museum. Agreement was recently reached between the owner of the farmstead and Bokrijk's open-air museum. This magnificent south Limburg "winning" will doubtless become one of the showpieces in the Haspengouw section of the museum.'*

The author didn't exaggerate. The Duifhuis from Bernissem with its severe, almost closed formation surrounding a central courtyard, and its unusually tall farmhouse is indeed one of the most remarkable features of the Haspengouw landscape. In 1663 and later – the actual date can be read in the metal wall ties of the farmhouse tower – it is clear that this building dominated the surrounding district in more ways than one. Like the Hooghuis from Tessenderlo, 12.1, in the Kempen, it had a pigeon tower where lesser tenants from the region were permitted to store their harvest. Certainly, the oldest part of the farmstead is the house tower where the openings can be seen through which the pigeons came and went. In the

18th and 19th centuries the lower part of the farmhouse was substantially rebuilt. It housed the sleeping quarters, the stable and the byre.

A curious architectural detail: the timber-framing in both the large and small barn isn't, as was normally the case, filled in with wattle and daub but with bricks and mortar. This type of construction is more widely found in the Voerstreek and the Ardennes, although in these regions it was more common to use natural stone in place of brick. In Limburg the amount of brickwork indicated the owner's wealth. Furthermore, those who could afford the initial outlay saved the cost of annual repairs to the half-timbering.

If when leaving the Duifhuis you follow the path you came along and then turn left, you will pass the large stone that marked the official boundary of Beverst, dated 1684 **11**, one of six boundary stones placed in 1684 to mark the border between Hoeselt and Beverst. The stones delineated the legal jurisdiction after the St Lambert chapter of Liège Cathedral became the landlords of Biesen, succeeding the German Order in Alden Biesen. The boundary stone shows the coat of arms of the Prince Bishop Maximilian of Bavaria, with two abbreviations standing for St Mary and St Lambert.

The octagonal Lady Chapel **12** just past the boundary stone dates from around 1700 and originates like the washhouse mentioned above from Ter Beek Abbey at Metsteren. It illustrates brotherly

The *Duifhuis* from Sint-Truiden-Bernissem

Wind mill from Schulen

integration, for the bell in the tower is from the chapel of St Anthony in Bree (1769) and the chapel's small altar is actually a side altar from the church of Erpekom (see no. 20, in the Kempen).

The small, simple and often impoverished farm labourer's dwellings, like the 19th-century whitewashed cottage here from Kortessem **13**, also have the typical layout of houses in south Limburg. There is a small entrance hall, also serving as mini threshing floor, leading into the kitchen and living room. This one has furniture made by a cabinetmaker from Genk in around 1900. Nowadays this type of house is very popular among urban dwellers as a holiday home. But its original inhabitants never had a holiday. Good to remember this when

Chapel of the *Ter Beek* abbey at Metsteren

ooking round the one in Bokrijk
hat's not for sale.

The museum bought a small
armstead from the village of Beverst
4.1 providing a fine illustration of
he way the quadrangular farmstead
gradually evolved in South Lim-
ourg. Built in 1783, dwelling and
barn share a single roof. Opposite
he dwelling is the cowshed with
he date in the lintel reading 1847.

Cottage from Kortessem

Farmstead from Beverst

The bakehouse was then built parallel to the byre and the square was completed with a row of pigsties on the south side. In the garden of the timber-frame house at Bokrijk a small bee house, originally from Alken, has been rebuilt **14.2**.

On the subject of smells: as was generally the case in these farms there was an open dunghill in the courtyard. But whereas in the Kempen, manure was about the most precious product of the farmyard, each drop jealousy guarded, in the fertile Haspengouw the liquid manure trickled across the yards and out into the streets. The soil was rich enough, it didn't need extra manure. So it won't surprise you to learn that impoverished farmers, especially from the Kempen, referred to the Haspengouwers, even though they were hardly much better off, as 'the stinking rich'. This expression has become well established in the Dutch language, but probably few people who use the term nowadays understand exactly why the rich, of all people, should stink. Now you know!

The museum has a long-gable farmhouse-inn from the village of Ulbeek, a half-timbered building dating from the 17th century **15.1**. As in days of yore, the food and drink served and the games played in this inn are typical of the Haspengouw region. Named *De Kleinaert,* after the place in Ulbeek where it stood three centuries long, the furnishings are those of a local Haspengouw country inn from the mid-19th century. Dwelling and commerce share one roof, which is partly tiled and partly thatched. In the lower part of the building are the barn, animal stalls and part of the kitchen, which also served as the bar. Halfway up the kitchen, at the level of the truss, another storey was constructed. Entry to the living area is via the typical hallway or *nere,* also used to access the rear of the house and the living rooms – in this case the kitchen-cum-alehouse and the 'best' room. Leading from the kitchen are an alcove and a small bedroom. In the second bay of the building, on the north side, is a storeroom and dairy. The buildings are completed by a byre and a small barn. When the house was reconstructed in Bokrijk, a small pigsty was placed adjoining the garden, originally belonging to the *Pachthof* at Kozen-Kortenbos **15.2**.

Farmhouse-inn from Ulbeek

Interior of the farmhouse-inn from Ulbeek

Interior of the cottage from Kortessem

Ulbeek village green; in the background the chapel from Zepperen

Beside the Ulbeek farmstead stands a chapel with a Baroque appearance, from the *Natte Bampt* or 'wet common grazing land' of Zepperen **16**. There is mention of this church as early as 1480, but its present appearance dates from 1736. The pulpit is particularly impressive, with its 'canopy' or 'roof' acting as an amplifier and projecting the speaker's voice. Here too, just as beside the church of the Kempen Erpekom (no.20 – from which incidentally there is an altar in this chapel), a small cemetery has been laid out. The crosses on the graves come, most appropriately, from south and central Limburg. And the strange thing is, there is a kind of presence in this graveyard, just as there is in the houses of Bokrijk – as if any moment the owner might appear when you are peeking into a cupboard or behind a curtain. Yet no one rests beneath these gravestones.

Chapel from the *Natte Bampt* of Zepperen

*Spijker* from Diepenbeek

The *Spijker* from Diepenbeek, the village school from Hoeselt and the chapel from Zepperen

The village school from Hoeselt and the chapel from Zepperen

You can already see it from the cemetery. Its Dutch name is *spijker,* or *spieker* from the late Latin word *spicarium,* meaning a storeroom. Not for all the tea in China would I live in such a place. But in past centuries it seemed an acceptable alternative – after all, you lived on the ground floor (with the attic above you groaning under the weight of the grain it stored). The *Spijker* from Diepenbeek **17** dating from the 16th or 17th century has corbelling between the ground floor roof and the attic. This gives it a solid sturdy beauty while at the same time providing a form of protection. On top of the protruding beams are sole pieces on which the wall posts of the attic stand. Via the corbels the horizontal pressure of the wall posts is transferred at an angle onto the vertical wall posts of the lower storey. Most ingenious, for without the corbelling the weight of the sacks of grain would inevitably push the lower walls out of sync. Living under the weight of harvest, a fascinating notion – I find the *Spijker* a thought-provoking landmark in the Bokrijk scene.

Equally fascinating, but then for a completely different reason, is the village school brought from the Limburg hamlet of Hoeselt **18**, where between 1905 and 1933 Anna-Maria Geridts held sway. The school's last teacher, she employed a learning-through-play method to guide her children through their early years, preparing them for elementary school where they would learn reading, writing and arithnetic, the holy trinity of the three R's. The school opened in 1886 and retains traces on the classroom wall from that highly nationalistic period of Belgian history. Here you can see the Belgian National Anthem which the children had to chant in chorus: *'No clod of Belgian earth shall e'er be wrenched from us, as long as Belgians live, be they Fleming or Walloon.'* A praiseworthy sentiment that was later to prove an illusion at times.

The half-timbered Hoeselt village school is probably the only surviving example of its kind in Flanders. The front of the building, however, was replaced with a brick wall. Inside the classroom memories flood back. People who started school before or shortly after World War II will recall vividly their early years as a pupil, half a century ago. Renovated according to the directions of former pupils, the scene is set as if the class were outside having playtime. The rows of desks each seating two children, the teacher's desk, the blackboard, chalk and cupboard, the wooden school satchels with their sliding lids, the iron stove all stands ready for the lesson to begin after break. On the wall hangs a list of the first one-syllable words children learn to read. A deeply nostalgic place for the older visitor, though for youngsters the 20th century is already ancient history. And completely a thing of the past is the bedroom so that the teacher could also live in the school building. Indeed, in Hoeselt this was the case. Don't imagine it was very comfortable or cosy – a table, a chest, a few chairs and a shelf in the kitchen, while the bedroom was furnished with a bed in rustic Empire style, a wardrobe and wooden shelves. The crowning glory was a Louvain stove, serving both as heater and cooker.

In 1928 Marieke (Anna-Maria) Geridts had some 30 infants in her

In the playground the little girls enjoyed games with a skipping rope and the boys played tug-o-war, and there were also marbles, jacks, skittles and spinning tops. These same games are organised today at Bokrijk for young visitors. Now that you're in the playground, take a look at the schoolteacher's toilet (in emergency directly accessible from the classroom) and the children's lavatories, for which the Dutch invented the expressive term *meerpersoonspoepdoos* (multi-person thunderbox). Even today toddlers and young children often sit on toilet bowls in a row, in crèches and kindergartens. But the British developments whereby toilets were connected to a sewage system and the whole procedure became more sophisticated, soon inspired the Continent. Adults began to attach greater importance to privacy when 'doing their daily job'. The companionable rows of toilets are still found in some places however, notably the Scandinavian countryside.

Meanwhile down the centuries farmers spread their own and their animals' droppings as manure to fertilise the soil. It was a long time before people appreciated the dangers inherent in this. Infected with micro-organisms the urine trickled into wells and polluted the drinking water. The result was typhus or (cesspit) fever. In the courtyard of the Beverst farmstead (no. 14.1) the drinking well is placed dangerously close to the dunghill – a clear illustration of people's ignorance about how diseases spread. It was thought that infections spread through putrid smells. Not until the 19th century was it known that the true cause of sickness is microscopic bacteria.

class. But then Mr Gielen arrived with the elementary-age children and the schoolmistress had to relocate with her brood to the living quarters of the schoolhouse. When she retired, Marieke continued to live in the schoolhouse until her death in 1969 at the splendid age of 101.

The classroom in the village school from Hoeselt

The *Paenhuys* from Diepenbeek

The majestic, somewhat chequered looking *Paenhuys* from Diepenbeek **19**, with its decorative cornice, probably dates from the 17th century. Since the name *paanhuis* or *pannehuis* is another word for brewery, when the house was reconstructed in Bokrijk it was based, following expert advice, on the layout of an artisanal brewery in Hoegaarden. Beer-lovers can reconstruct the whole process from malt to foaming drink, from the hop boiler to the fermentation tank. Until the French Revolution people were required to buy their beer or have it brewed in this Paenhuys. This gave the local officials more control over the beer taxes. Indeed, the import of beer was forbidden on various estates, unless the vats were checked by the local tax inspector.

On the other side of the street stands the reconstruction of a small farmstead, dismantled from the northern part of Haspengouw. It comprises a dwelling from Kortessem **20.1**, a pigsty from Schakkebroek **20.2** and a bakehouse from Zolder-Viversel **20.3**. As an exception this house from the 18th and early 19th centuries isn't divided into the typical kitchen and living room. Via the central kitchen you reach the storeroom and two small bedrooms. The interior has been furnished with loving care, just as the last inhabitant would have known it in around 1890. There is a large fireplace, a simple table and bench, a cupboard with traditional decoration and here and there a few knick-knacks. A photograph of the house's last owner and inhabitant, Jan Claesen, hangs in the hall. He died in 1955, just two years after he had said farewell to his house in a verse containing passages from a poem he had learnt at school. This is what he wrote:

*Farewell to my old house where*
*    I lived from 25 March 1874 and*
*        left in 1953, on 7 November.*
*My house was neither large nor grand*
*Yet was my shelter in this land.*
*Indeed it was but poor and small*
*Yet warmly welcomed one and all.*
*Thus in my thoughts and in my*
*        dreams*
*It better than a palace seems.*
*So here I'll stay with all my wares*
*For mighty mansions only bring*
*        mighty cares.*

Mighty mansions, mighty problems. These words express understanding of the age-old wisdom that money can't buy happiness.

Dwelling from Kortessem

Interior of the dwelling from Kortessem

Long-gable farmhouse from Sint-Martens-Voeren

Boundery marker from Hasselt

The little street beside Jan Claesen's house leads to a farmhouse from the Voerstreek, built around 1700 **21**. About 250 years later it closed its doors to its last inhabitant, a solitary woman who avoided human company. The farmstead is a perfect example of the local building techniques of those days. The front is timber framed, in this case using sturdy oak beams to produce a grid effect with openings left for the small windows. We find similar techniques used in the Maasland, the area around Eupen and Malmedy, the Rhineland and Dutch Limburg. What makes the Voerstreek different is the presence of flint, from which the side and rear walls are made. This farmhouse in Sint-Martens-Voeren lay on a clay plateau above a chalk valley, and the effect of erosion was to uncover a layer of flint. Furthermore there was plenty of wood available on the hillsides, so that flint and wood became the chief building materials of the region. If you have the good luck to spend some time in the beautiful countryside of Voeren, don't miss the plateau of Sint-Martens-Voeren. (And keep an eye out for the many delightful half-timbered and flint restaurants.) Here, close to where the farm now in Bokrijk once stood, you are at the highest point in Flanders, roughly 287 metres (about 1,000 feet) above sea level.

On the other side of Jan Claesen's house is a pillar chapel that comes from Brustem and a memorial stone cross from Veulen **23**. It once marked the spot on the Veulen road where in 1791, so we learn, Mistress Lucia Greven, widow of Mathys Thevis, suddenly died. On the same side of the road, going towards the Kempen, is a boundary stone from 1666 bearing a coat of arms **25**. It was here that the illustrious Prince Bishop Maximilian Henry of Bavaria threatened the people of Zonhoven with dire punishment should they dare to allow their cattle to graze in the Hasselt meadows on the other side of the boundary stone. Barbed wire hadn't been invented, corporal punishment was still the order of the day.

Nearby was an 18th-century octagonal tower windmill from Schulen **26** with huge wooden beams inside. Unfortunately the mill couldn't catch enough wind to turn the sails. But to give it the chance to show that if it had enough wind it could function efficiently, it was dismantled and reconstructed on the other side of the hill, opposite the Ter Beek chapel. With this type of windmill, familiarly known as a coffeepot mill, only the cap can turn into the wind. This is done using a set of beams stretching from the cap to the ground and linked to the mechanism. From other sources describing the mechanism of such windmills we learn that 'the crown-wheel of the main post uses wallowers to drive the upper millstone or 'runner' and that 'in the hoist-loft the main post supports a platform to which the hoist mechanism can be connected by means of a friction wheel'. I suspect that true windmill lovers know this already and refer those who desire a little more tech-

nical information to the bibliography at the end of this booklet.

## BRABANT

Belgian Brabant is also situated in the fertile uplands. This province too has several types of agricultural land which in times gone by were exploited by the great abbeys (such as Nijvel, Grimbergen and Affligem) and their tenants in this district.

And in Brabant also various shapes of farmsteads were built – some with all the rooms behind one long gable, some with several separate buildings and above all large leasehold quadrangular farms with an entirely closed construction. There are still magnificent examples of such buildings in the Pajottenland and Hageland districts.

So far the gleanings from Brabant that have arrived in Bokrijk are limited to the base of a freestanding pigeon tower in Eppegem (Zemst) **27**. This once stood in the castle farm of the *Indevelde* estate, where it was built in the heart of the grounds between 1624 and 1627. The tower itself is missing, otherwise you would have been able to see the openings through which the pigeons came and went on their missions. Eppegem was formerly home to a vast number of pigeons, having no less than 1100 nests in the tower. The remains of the former palace of pigeons stand at the side of the road when you leave the Schulen windmill (no. 26, in Haspengouw) walking in the direction of the Old Town.

Bakehouse from Loppem

I come from the Meetjesland of eastern Flanders so it's a bit of a disappointment to me that the museum in Bokrijk has not one example of a building from this remarkable flat polder land. But there are extenuating circumstances. Not surprisingly, the people who constructed Bokrijk went back to their own roots, their *bakermat* or origins, in Limburg. Then they looked at neighbouring and in many ways related cultivated areas such as large parts of Haspengouw and the Antwerp Kempen, or poor moorlands. Furthermore, Jozef Weyns the curator clearly had better connections in West Flanders than he had in East Flanders. So East Flanders gets a raw deal, represented with only one large house, a couple of dyke houses, a barn and a small number of storerooms.

A raw deal, but not total disregard. For despite my chauvinistic outburst above I can recommend most warmly the Bokrijk route through East and West Flanders. In fact, I'd like to suggest that this particular walk, with its widely scattered farmsteads, its many open spaces and pleasant copses, this amble though the fertile lowlands is perhaps the loveliest in the entire open-air museum. In contrast to the sections presenting the Kempen moorland and the Haspengouw uplands, this part doesn't have a central settlement but has the houses, barns and cowsheds scattered around within easy walking distance of each other. This is the freshest and most invigorating place in the whole of Bokrijk.

The style of farmhouse building in East and West Flanders uses chiefly separate constructions, sometimes grouped in a U-shape, sometimes in a square surrounding a courtyard. There were moated farmsteads and farms fringed with high hedges of beech or hawthorn, usually mixed with pollard willows. Here again we find the long-gabled farmstead but it differs from those in the Kempen both in structure, size and general architecture. Building materials differ from region to region – the timber-framing technique is much used, as in northern France and southern England, in Belgium's Westhoek and in parts of East Flanders; while in the polders of Bruges and Antwerp, as in large parts of West Flanders, there is predominantly brick and mortar.

Wagon house from Ardooie

Bakehouse from Watou

The date 1771 is chiselled into the lintel of the door with the architect's initials, 'PB'. Petrus Bouquet's farmhouse **1.1** lay in Abele (Poperinge) just a few steps away from what was locally known as the *schreve*, the boundary with France. No one from those parts knows why the house was named *Het Paddekot* – a guess is that it was a bastardisation of a French name. Everyone, however, understands why it was called a *hommelhofstede*, or hop-house. From as early as the 16th century we find the word *hommel* used for hop and in the Poperinge district hop growing was a major industry. It was a challenging means of livelihood, and not only because of the outdoor aspects. Possibly the most demanding part of hop production was the drying process, involving turning the plants on a drying floor. The labourers would often have to work between eleven and thirteen hours at a stretch, crouched in a stifling room in suffocating smoke, until the hops were completely dry. Not surprisingly they used the word 'hell' to refer to the drying room in the oast house (and, incidentally, the autumnal storms that blew down the bunches of hops were known as 'hop devils').

Today in Bokrijk the house from Abele stands quiet and serene with no scenes of an inferno. A curious detail is that only the kitchen is heated, not the living room. We know from other houses in this neighbourhood that there was almost always a double fireplace built between the kitchen and living space. Possibly the most interesting room in the whole house is the cellar. Not only is it exceptionally large, it also has windows. It was used to store food, and perhaps also housed the weaving loom. A dry cellar in fact. Just as in many houses in the Kempen and Haspengouw, here too the cellars were always built above the ground-water level. Thus we find low dry cellars with an *opkamer* or room built above them. These were on joists and higher than the other rooms on the same floor – an extremely thrifty form of space saving.

In the second half of the 19th century almost all the timber-frame buildings in the district were replaced by brick and mortar. The cowshed dating from about mid-18th century from Oostcappel **1.2**, just over the French border, is one of the last surviving timber-frame structures. It includes a cowstall, a wagon shed and an 18th-century stable which appears to have been added later. A small touch worth noting – in the main beam in the stable-roof truss one of the stable lads, called I.F. Coolen, carved his name artistically inside a flower motif. Presumably he slept in the stables and wanted to record his presence in this way.

In the same magnificent farmstead compound there is also a rare half-timbered barn from Proven in West Flanders **1.3**. The graffiti on the posts at the side of the threshing floor reveal that the barn dates from the early 17th century. The floor,

which is covered with a layer of clay, lies right across the length of the building and is bordered by planking so that stray pieces of grain wouldn't slip down into the storeroom during the threshing process.

When the grain was being threshed by hand it must have been extremely difficult to breathe. But far more barbaric was the fate of labourers in the drying rooms, nicknamed 'hop furnaces'. You can see the shape of an upside-down pyramid in the walls of the drying oven from Proven **1.4**, which is a closed-off air vent. It conducted the hot air above to where the hops lay on a rack. There was a layer about 20 or 30 centimetres deep which had to be turned regularly. Without a chimney, the building is nothing short of an inferno.

It must also have got pretty hot inside the bakehouse of Watou **1.5** but at least that had a chimney in its tiled roof. The wagons, the three-wheeled cart, the ladders, rakes and harrows and ploughs all fitted into the wagon shed, of which you see a fine example here from Leisele **1.6**.

Originally, semidetached dwellings would have been the homes of poor peasants. Most of them, however, developed into dwellings for one family. The pair of half-timbered cottages from Oostvleteren **2.1** probably dates from the second half of the 18th century. The former curator Weyns made a mistake in his interpretation of the dating on a beam in the room. The inscription reads ANO XVeVIJ (=1507) and he wrote gleefully in his book that *'this house is not only the oldest preserved wattle-and-daub farmhouse in West Flanders, it is – as far as is known – the oldest such building in the entire Netherlands.'* But unfortunately research showed that when the house was constructed older elements were reused.

Inside the simple yet inviting house you can see objects such as a kneading trough table, the complete toolkit of a chairmaker and on the left beside the large fireplace, a mustard mill. In those days mustard was a widely used condiment, smothering in large quantities eggs and beans that had been preserved for months, in an attempt to conceal the sour and bitter taste. Mustard was also a welcome addition, particularly in the time of Lent, to a meal of dried fish or herring. The farmer's wife would put the mustard seed into a wooden bowl together with a cannonball. Then she would shake the bowl between her knees so that the heavy ball crushed the seeds as it rolled. This mustard mill produced far more mustard powder than the family needed. So husband or chil-

dren would trundle the mustard through the streets, maybe transporting it in a pony and trap. We know that the last person to live in this house, Maria Vandecasteele, still ground her mustard in a bowl between her knees, while at the same time, she claimed, doing her knitting or crochet. The widow of Jules Mazereel, she lived in the house for over 50 years. When she died the words on the prayer card read: *'Much has been said about her house and everyone who lived in the neighbourhood was keen to see it. . . then it was pulled down to be rebuilt far away, in greater glory than at first.'*

At the time that the house was pulled down the servants' dwellings had already gone from the compound. So when it was reconstructed in Bokrijk the complex was completed by adding a mid-16th-century winter barn from Vinkem **2.2**, a horse-mill from Leisele dating from 1861 **2.3** and a wagon shed from Beveren-aan-den-IJzer **2.4**.

A word about the horse mill. Its name explains it – the mill was driven by horsepower. The horse plodded endlessly around a central axle pulling the machinery. It was common to have horse-driven mills near windmills. Then if there was no wind, horsepower would be used. But as early as the First World War most of the horse-drawn mills had disappeared, partly because the German troops demanded the animals for less peaceable purposes, partly with the arrival of diesel and electric engines.

Farmhouse from Oostvleteren

Farmhouse from Loppem

Wagon shed from Beveren-aan-den-IJzer

Farmhouse from Hoogstade

he farmhouse from Hoogstade **3.1** with its villa-like appearance, formerly belonged to the abbey of ...versam. The building lay on the ...ver IJzer and the tenant could earn ...he odd cent ferrying people across ...he water. Like many such farm-...teads in the district this building, ...hen dating to the 16th century, ...as razed to the ground by French ...roops at the end of the 18th centu-

ry. Not long after, it was rebuilt, and the distinguished house you now see in Bokrijk dates from then. Inside too the atmosphere speaks of the bourgeoisie. One of the show-pieces is the longcase clock, inside which the gentleman-farmer kept his walking stick. On the inside of its door he listed the dates when his cows and sows were served, noting their names.

Horse mill from Lampernisse and swingle barn from Leisele

Horse mill from Lampernisse

The barn with the impressive pyramidal thatch roof **3.2** belonged to the abbey of Lo, a small town in West Flanders. This is inscribed on a post at the side of the threshing floor: +1715. DESE MECK[E] BEHOORT [T]OE AEN DAB[DY] [V]AN LOO. Although the date is given as 1715, the barn was probably older. The word *mecke* is the West Flanders dialect term for this type of barn. They are very similar to those in Frisia but there seems to be no direct connection between the building styles. The sides of the square barn measure a good 14 metres each. Inside this simple but highly efficient cube the farmer stored his grain. The grain would be ground using the horse-drawn mill while a connection with a butter churn ensured that the cream was

Horse mill from Lampernisse and the barn from Lo

imultaneously turned into butter
the example here, from Lamper-
isse **3.3**, dates from the 19th centu-
y). The carts would be housed each
ight in a wagon house (the one
ere comes from Ardooie and dates
rom 1743 **3.4**), while in the swingle
arn (the one here is from Leisele
**.5**) the swingle – a flat-bladed
vooden instrument – was used
o beat and scrape the flax.

Farm labourers' cottages from Meulebeke

Crossing the museum's section of West Flanders you come upon a whitewashed 18th-century Lady Chapel from Rollegem-Kapelle **10** and shortly after almost bump into a pigeon tower from Ingelmunster **4** built in 1634 in the grounds of its fortified farmstead. This isn't a building to ignore. A pigeon tower was a status symbol, both architecturally and for its contents. The towers differed from district to district in their outward appearance but inside were more or less the same. The ground floor housed poultry or pigs, fodder was stored on the first floor, and the pigeon nests were at the top. The only way to reach the top storey of the Ingelmunster tower was by ladder – an attempt to hinder people from stealing the chicks who were to be

Pigeon tower from Ingelmunster

Barn from Zuienkerke

the future post birds and fancy
pigeons and doves.

   Nearby stands a row of simple
terraced farm labourers' cottages
from Meulebeke **6** in central West
Flanders. In one of the attic rafters
someone with a sense of history has
carved the date 1767. The front door
leads straight into the house, that is,
the kitchen, but the bedroom lies at
the rear, while the room adjoining
the kitchen probably once held the
weaving loom. In the frequently
rebuilt barn, brought from the polder land of Bruges **7** and used for storage and stables – the earliest reference to it, incidentally, dates from
1333 – visitors may well imagine
they are standing in a rustic cathedral. The barn formed part of the
*Schoeringe* farmstead in Zuienkerke
near Bruges. The core of the barn
comprises four imposing trusses
each one with a double-curved brace
to strengthen the construction. The
entire truss section is anchored into
stones which are in turn secured two
metres deep in the ground. Unlike
the construction in the Kempen
where the pressure is born by the
purlins and the wall-plates, here the
vast weight of the roof is born by
the central pillars. A masterpiece of
building.

   But as it has always been the
whole world over, riches weren't
evenly spread – it often depended
on the quality of the land where you
lived. Down the centuries countless
small tenant farmers and manual
workers lived in simple wattle-and-
daub houses on the poor sandy soil
around Bruges. One such house
from Loppem **8.1**, dating from 1735,
can be seen here. It might once have
been one of a pair of cottages, later
becoming a home for only one family. Barn and cowshed are from the
same site. But the bakehouse **8.2** is a
little too grand to have belonged to
poor peasants.

   In order to have a brief pause we
return to the Westhoek, or to be

Barn from Zuienkerke

Farmhouse from Loppem

more precise to the old town hall of St Rijkers **9** that already served as a tavern in the 19th century. The inn, called *In den Dolphin* (the latter word coming from the French *dauphin,* meaning crown prince), is built from the characteristic yellow brick of the Veurne woodlands. Inside looks all too familiar – two rooms and a semi-basement with cellar room. The tavern has a kind of bowling alley, called a *bolderbaan*. The *bol* game used to be hugely popular in Flemish cafes. It looks easier than it really is. The players have a large disk which – and here's the tricky part of it – is weighted on one side, and try to roll it as close as possible to a peg or the 'goal'. Even today this game is widely played, especially on Sundays and on particular holidays.

## 11

Farmhouse-inn-village hall *In den Dolphin* from Sint-Rijkers

As visitors have discovered by now, there's no shortage of stone monuments to the Virgin Mary in Bokrijk. The chapel from Kortemark 11 was dedicated to Our Lady of Consolation. Such an outpouring of piety along the route might seem too much of a good thing. In fact, it's Bokrijk being true to its commitment to represent the countryside of Belgium as it used to be. For the enthusiast has yet to be born who will undertake to count all the Lady Chapels that once lay scattered along the highways and byways of Flanders.

Chapel from Rollegem-Kapelle

Barn from Oorderen

The barn **12** which has belonged since the mid-18th century to the *Berghoeve* farmstead of Oorderen measures some 32 by 19.5 metres and stands 13 metres high, making it the largest old barn of its type in the Antwerp polder. In Bokrijk this colossus offers a roof to a motley collection of interesting old vehicles – handcart, pony and trap, bicycles, beer cart, all kinds of four-wheelers, carriages, phaetons and chaises, indeed there is even a hearse, journey's end. A sobering moment before you tear off down the highway.

At right angles to the barn stands a typical 19th-century polder stable for animals and carts from the village of Kallo on the River Scheldt, the Antwerp Left Bank. Further along are two dyke houses also

Cowshed and wagon shed from Kallo

coming from Kallo, in the 19th century **13**. Both have a lean-to, one
built in brick, the other in wood. In
the first house the barber trims and
shaves his clients in the living room.
Beside the mirror hangs his list of
prices. You can also see the razor,
strop, shaving bowls and shaving
stone, or alum – incidentally still an
excellent means of staunching small
cuts from shaving.

The other dyke house was a
labourer's dwelling. Nowadays a
young couple will leave a house this
size when they have their first or
second child. But at the beginning of
the 1900s a couple called Ludovicus
Lichtert and Maria De Vos lived
there with their 13 children. Probably the little ones slept, as was common then, with five of them cross-
ways in the bed, maybe a couple of

Dyke house from Kallo

children had a box as a cradle, the older boys were perhaps in the stable or the attic, and a couple of the girls in the basement. In those days there was no whisper in Catholic Flanders of such a thing as contraception, nor were there child allowances or scholarships for studying. Ludovicus and Maria's children never went to school. While still young they got jobs as cowherd or servant on the great estates, where they received both board and keep.

Such crowded living was also characteristic of the only farmhouse dwelling from East Flanders at Bokrijk **14.1**. In about the mid-19th century this typical house from Lokeren in the Waasland was home to no fewer people than: Jacob De Vriendt, his sister Coleta, her daughter Natalia with her husband and 12 children. Apart from certain architectural details (for example the dormer providing light to the attic and the section of the basement that intrudes into the space occupied by the living room) what is particularly striking about this house is its fireplace. It originally adorned a dwelling in Elversele, and presents a splendid tableau in blue and sepia Delft tiles showing scenes from the Bible. The large barn **14.2** dating from the early 18th century also comes from Lokeren, while the bakery – probably of a later date **14.3** is from nearby Waasmunster.

In 1895 the stone pillar chapel from Meerbeke in East Flanders **15** was placed on the spot where a flax dealer had suddenly dropped dead.

The text on it reads IN HONOREM BEATAE MARIAE VIRGINIS (To the honour of the Blessed Virgin Mary) because it is she who intercedes in heaven for the souls of those who are so unfortunate as to die before they can receive the last Sacrament. This means no final absolution for their sins – so Mary is the only hope.

Side wall of the house from Lokeren

Transverse barn from Lokeren

Bokrijk wouldn't be Bokrijk if we didn't end up in Limburg at the end of our walk. Though it's quite by chance. What happened was that before the East Flanders section was extended a copy was made in this part of the grounds of a Kempen entrenchment with a simple dwelling from Beverlo **16**.

This type of entrenchment would have been used in times of trouble, as when marauding gangs, sometimes of unpaid soldiers, roamed and plundered the region. In Haspengouw people sought refuge in the strong stone-built farmsteads or fortified strongholds but for the poor farmers of the Kempen, apart from a few walled cities like Bree, Peer and Hamont, there was no safe place. So arose the custom of building a *schans* or entrenchment in outlying areas. This went as follows: a moat would be dug out around a plot of land sometimes as large as one hectare, and then ramparts built using the dug-out earth, reinforced with wood and wattle and daub. Sometimes there would be a drawbridge at the entrance, and a gateway. In times of trouble the villagers would hurry there with their provisions – food and household goods. And then pray that the brigands wouldn't be trained soldiers but just a disorganised band of robbers.

You can see the remains of these entrenchments in various parts of the Kempen. The one in Bokrijk is a copy of the *Molenvenseschans* from Haspershoven (Overpelt).

Farmhouse from Beverlo

## Epilogue

A strange thing happened to me as I was walking through the open-air museum of Bokrijk. It's perfectly normal to imagine you see people in many of the houses – eating, working, sleeping, going about their daily lives. The curious thing was – in all the old houses I only saw old people.

Maybe you've had a similar experience. So I conclude with some statistics.

At the turn of the 20th century the average life expectancy of a man in Flanders was 74.6 years, and that of a woman 80.6 years. Due to various factors, including high infant mortality, inadequate medicine, epidemics and so forth, the average life expectancy in Flanders in the mid-17th century was 25 years. Towards the close of the 18th century average life expectancy had risen to 30 years. By 1850 people living in the Limburg Kempen as far as the Westhoek had a life expectancy of 36 years, and by 1900 this had risen to 45 years.

What I mean to say is – as you walk around Bokrijk, you won't come across many old people haunting the old houses.

Sawpit

Interior of the cottage from Kortessem

M. BOONE, H. GAUS, P. SCHOL-
LIERS and C. VANDENBROEKE,
*Dagelijks leven. Sociaal-culturele
omstandigheden vroeger en nu.*
In: Culturele geschiedenis
van Vlaanderen 10, Deurne-
Ommen, 1982.
BRUGGEMAN, CONTANT,
DENEWET et. al., *Travailler au
moulin/Werken met molens,*
published by ARAM Nord/
Pas-de-Calais & Werkgroep
West-Vlaamse Molens vzw,
1996.
E. DE VROEDE, *Het grote volks-
sporten boek,* Louvain, 1996.
E. DE VROEDE and B. EELBODE,
*Spele weerom: kinderspel van
alle tijden,* Kapellen, 1986.
*Kinderen van alle tijden. Kindercul-
tuur in de Nederlanden vanaf de
Middeleeuwen tot heden.* exhibi-
tion catalogue, North Brabant
Museum, Den Bosch, 28 March-
6 July 1997.
M. LAENEN, *Provinciaal Open-
luchtmuseum Bokrijk,* Brussels-
Bokrijk, 1982.
M. LAENEN, *Openluchtmuseum
Bokrijk* In: Cultura Nostra.
Musea in België, Brussels-Tielt,
1986.
M. LAENEN, *Openluchtmusea,
verleden, heden en toekomst,* n.p.,
n.d.
P. LINDEMANS, *Geschiedenis van de
landbouw,* Antwerpen: Het
Genootschap voor Geschiedenis
en Volkskunde, 1974.
G. TACK, P. VAN DEN BREMPT, M.
HERMY, *Bossen in Vlaanderen.
Een historische ecologie,* Davids-
fonds, Louvain, 1993.

CLEMENS V. TREFOIS, *Van vak-
werkbouw tot baksteenbouw,*
Sint-Niklaas, 1979.
G.VANDENBOSCH, *Hemel, hel en
vagevuur. Preken over het
hiernamaals in de Zuidelijke
Nederlanden tijdens de 17de en
18de eeuw,* Louvain, 1991.
G. VAN DEN BRINCK, *De grote
overgang. Woensel 1670-1920.
Een lokaal onderzoek naar de
modernisering van het bestaan,*
Nijmegen, 1996.
J. VAN HAVER, *Voor U beminde
gelovigen. Het rijke roomse Leven
in Vlaanderen 1920-1950,* Tielt,
1995.
ROBERTSON A. UNA, *The Illustrat-
ed History of the Housewife
1650-1950,* Gloucestershire,
1997.
J. WEYNS, *Omstandige gids van het
Openluchtmuseum te Bokrijk,*
1967.
J. WEYNS, *Volkshuisraad in Vlaanderen. Naam, vorm, geschiedenis,
gebruik en volkskundig belang
der huishoudelijke voorwerpen in
het Vlaamse Land van de Middeleeuwen tot de Eerste Wereld-
oorlog,* Beerzel, 1974.

Journals

*Biekorf: Westvlaams archief voor
Geschiedenis, archeologie, taal-
en volkskunde,* Bruges 1890–
*Continuity and Change. A Journal of
Social Structure, Law and
Demography in Past Societies,*
New Orleans, Louisiana, 70118-
5670.
*Eigen Schoon en de Brabander:
Driemaandelijks tijdschrift van
het Koninklijk Geschied- en Oud-
heidkundig Genootschap van
Vlaams-Brabant,* Brussels,
1948–
*Historische Anthropologie. Kultur –
Gesellschaft – Alltag,* heraus-
gegeben von Ute Luig, Edith
Saueder und Rolf Lindner,
Cologne 1993–
*Ons Heem: mededelingen van het
Verbond voor Heemkunde,*
Heist-op-den-Berg, Verbond
voor Heemkunde, 1947–
*Oost-Vlaamse Zanten: tijdschrift
voor volkscultuur in Vlaanderen,*
Gent, Koninklijke Bond der
Oostvlaamse Volkskundigen,
1926–
*Taxandria: jaarboek van de Konink-
lijke geschied- en oudheidkundige
kring van de Antwerpse
Kempen,*Turnhout 1939–

© 2001 Ludion Ghent-Amsterdam & Laurens De Keyzer
© 2001 Michiel Hendryckx
Design: Antoon De Vylder, Herentals
Typesetting: De Diamant Pers, Herentals
Translation: Lynn George and Wendie Shaffe
Editing: First Edition, Cambridge
Colour separations and printing: Die Keure, Bruges
D/2001/6328/25
ISBN: 90-5544-335-2